Moorcroft

Inspired by Stories of a Scottish Working-Class Community

Eilidh Loan

methuen | drama

LONDON • NEW YORK • OXFORD • NEW DELHI • SYDNEY

METHUEN DRAMA
Bloomsbury Publishing Plc
50 Bedford Square, London, WC1B 3DP, UK
1385 Broadway, New York, NY 10018, USA
29 Earlsfort Terrace, Dublin 2, Ireland

BLOOMSBURY, METHUEN DRAMA and the Methuen
Drama logo are trademarks of Bloomsbury Publishing Plc

First published in Great Britain 2023

Cover image featuring Martin Docherty as Garry

Cover design: thisisjamhot.com

Photography by Joe Connolly

A catalogue record for this book is available from the British Library.

A catalog record for this book is available from the Library of Congress.

ISBN: PB: 978-1-3504-4163-7
ePDF: 978-1-3504-4164-4
eBook: 978-1-3504-4165-1

Series: Modern Plays

Typeset by Mark Heslington Ltd, Scarborough, North Yorkshire

To find out more about our authors and books visit
www.bloomsbury.com and sign up for our newsletters.

Tron Theatre Company presents

Moorcroft

by Eilidh Loan

Moorcroft was first performed at the Tron Theatre, Glasgow on Thursday 17 February 2022

Moorcroft was remounted at the Tron Theatre, Glasgow on Thursday 13 July 2023 and toured Scotland in autumn 2023, in association with the National Theatre of Scotland

ALBA | CHRUTHACHAIL

Original Company Credits Tron Theatre 2022

CAST in alphabetical order

PAUL	**Sean Connor**
GARRY	**Martin Docherty**
SOOTY	**Kyle Gardiner**
TUBS	**Ryan Hunter**
MINCE	**Martin Quinn**
MICK	**Jatinder Singh Randhawa**
NOODLES	**Santino Smith**

Writer & Director	**Eilidh Loan**
Set & Costume Design	**Carys Hobbs**
Lighting Design	**Michaella Fee**
Composer & Sound Design	**Gary Cameron**
Dramaturgical Support	**Johnny McKnight**
Stage Manager	**Astrid Rothmeier**
Deputy Stage Manager	**Cathy O'Neill**
Assistant Stage Manager	**Rebecca Romano Bell**
Costume Supervisor	**Victoria Brown**
Production Manager	**Laura Walshe**
Technical Manager	**Mark Hughes**
Technical Stage Manager	**Jason McQuaide**
Venue Technician	**Odhran Duignan**
Set Construction	**Pretty Scenic**
Scenic Artist	**Mischa Zielinska**

Remount Company Credits 2023

CAST in alphabetical order

PAUL	**Sean Connor**
GARRY	**Martin Docherty**
SOOTY	**Kyle Gardiner**
MINCE	**Bailey Newsome**
MICK	**Jatinder Singh Randhawa**
NOODLES	**Santino Smith**
TUBS	**Dylan Wood**

Writer & Director	**Eilidh Loan**
Set & Costume Design	**Carys Hobbs**
Lighting Design	**Michaella Fee**
Composer & Sound Design	**Gary Cameron**
Dramaturgical Support	**Johnny McKnight**
Associate Director	**Santino Smith**
Assistant Director	**Stephanie Austin**
Stage Manager	**Suzanne Goldberg**
Deputy Stage Manager	**Bryan Gallagher**
Assistant Stage Manager	**Zeni Bollok**
Costume Supervisor	**Victoria Brown**
Production Manager	**Laura Walshe**
Technical Manager	**Mark Hughes**
Technical Stage Manager	**Jason McQuaide**
Venue Technician	**Alex Hatfield**
Venue Technician	**Craig Crawford**
Set Construction	**Pretty Scenic**

THE COMPANY

EILIDH LOAN (Writer & Director)

Eilidh Loan is an award-winning actor, writer and director from Renfrewshire. In 2018, Eilidh graduated the Guildford School of Acting as the winner of the Bachelor of the Arts Acting Prize, the GSA Entrepreneur Award and as a finalist in the BBC Carleton Hobbs Bursary Competition. In her graduating year, Eilidh won the prestigious Alan Bates Competition, beating over 200 applicants from drama schools across the UK. She has gone on to make a successful career across all areas of the industry.

Eilidh was nominated for Best Writer at the Stage Debut Awards and for two CATS Awards in 2022 for Moorcroft. She was selected as one of The Scotsman's 'Ones to Watch 2023'.

Eilidh was awarded the New York City Radio Award for directing, creating and performing in, *Two Bad Mice* for Almost Tangible. Since then, Eilidh has continued to work closely with the company, gaining a nomination for Best Actress in a drama at the One Voice Awards for her portrayal of Lady Macbeth in the five-time award-winning production of *Macbeth*.

Eilidh wrote, directed and starred in her debut short film, *Soul* that was selected by Screen Scotland and BFI, Short Sharps programme.

Eilidh has recently appeared in Molly Manning Walker's hit feature film *How to Have Sex* and has also been cast in the new series of *Doctor Who*.

Her other credits include: *A Castle for Christmas* (Netflix); *Traces 2*, *The Sister Boniface Mysteries*, *Pancake*, *Clique 2*, *Doctors*, *England's Forgotten Queen* (BBC); *London Kills* (Acorn TV); *Doctor Who* (Big Finish); *Frankenstein* (UK tour); *Mary & Ada Set the World To Rights* (Óran Mòr); *Me and My Left Ball*

(Tristan Bates) and *Me and My Sister Tell Each Other Everything* (Tron Theatre).

GARY CAMERON (Composer & Sound Design)

Gary is a Glasgow-based sound designer and composer for stage and screen. His extensive and eclectic specialism in audio creation has been heard in over seventy productions across the UK and Europe. As resident composer with Folksy Theatre, Gary has composed songs and score for the works of Julia Donaldson and Quentin Blake amongst others. Gary is also the Director of the award-winning Dumfries Community Choir.

Selected credits include: *Inside Culture* (BBC); *Moorcroft* (Tron Theatre); *The Steamie, The Love of the Nightingale* (Dundee Rep); *Common Man, Tin Forest* (National Theatre of Scotland); *Educating Rita* (Perth/Horsecross); *Fuse, Quota* (Festival Theatre); *Pig* (Hull Truck Theatre); *Don Jon* (Silent Uproar); *25 Live, Lysistrata* (Capital Theatres); *Us and Them, A Midsummer Night's Dream* (Royal Lyceum); *Santa's Little Astronaut, Is That You, Santa? Eric the Elf* (Macrobert Arts Centre); *Mitzi the House Mouse, There's a Mouse in the House, Let the Light In* (Cumbernauld Theatre); *Tank* (Manipulate); *The Headland* (Mull Theatre); *Many Voices* (Scottish Parliament TV); *Puss in Boots* (Hopscotch Theatre); *Cinderella* (Bard In The Botanics); *The Happiness Formula* (Scottish Youth Theatre) and many more.

SEAN CONNOR (Paul)

Sean Connor is an actor based in Glasgow, Scotland. He graduated from New College Lanarkshire with a Bachelor of Arts Honours degree in acting in 2017 and has since appeared in numerous film and television projects, including: *Schemers* (Black Factory Films, 2020); *Still Game* (BBC1, 2019); *Traces* (Alibi, 2022). He is best known for playing series regular Dylan Christie in BBC Scotland's hit soap *River City*. His theatre credits include *Sean and Daro Flake It 'Til They Make It* (Traverse Theatre); *Until It's Gone* (Òran Mór); *Moorcroft* (Tron Theatre); *Ode to Joy* (Stories Untold Productions @ Ed Fringe) and *Don Quixote: Man of Clackmannanshire* (Dundee Rep and Perth Theatre).

MARTIN DOCHERTY (Garry)

Martin has previously appeared at the Tron Theatre in: *Risk, Club Asylum, Antigone* and *Cooking with Elvis*. Other theatre credits include: *Venice Preserved, Snow White, Scarfed for Life, Whatever Happened to the Jaggy Nettles* and *Annville* (Citizens Theatre); *Continuous Growth, Preen Back Yer Lugs, The Year of the Hare* (People's Theatre of Finland); *Nasty Brutish and Short* (Traverse Theatre); *Thieves and Boy* (Óran Mòr); *The Three Estates* (Edinburgh University); *Stitchers* (Jermyn Street Theatre); *The Hard Man* (Finborough Theatre) and *The Invisible Hand* (Kirkcaldy For All). In 2018 Martin and Martin Travers co-wrote and produced *McLuckie's Line*, a one man show which toured Scotland.

Television credits include: *Still Game, Dear Green Place, Rab C. Nesbitt, River City, One Night In Emergency, Gary Tank Commander, Young James, Case Histories, Father Brown, Outlander* and *The Demon Headmaster*. Feature film credits include: *Cloud Atlas, Filth* and *Country Music*. A documentary featuring Martin called *Marty Goes to Hollywood* won a New Talent BAFTA in 2015.

MICHAELLA FEE (Lighting Design)

Michaella is a theatrical lighting designer based in Glasgow. She trained at the Royal Conservatoire of Scotland which she graduated from in 2010. Since then, she has worked and collaborated with many artists and companies, mostly based in Scotland. She is particularly interested in contemporary performance and use of bold lighting. Her recent credits include *Childminder*, written by Iain McClure and directed by

Kolbrún Björt Sigfúsdóttir; *Ballad of the Apathetic Boy and His Narcissistic Mother* (21 Common); *Solway to Svalbard* by Stuart MacPherson; *Ginger* (Tortoise in a Nutshell); *Stuntman* (Superfan); *Grin* at Battersea Arts Centre by Mele Broomes; *Remedy for Memory* by Tess Letham and *Me and My Sister Tell Each Other Everything* (Tron Theatre).

KYLE GARDINER (Sooty)

Kyle is a graduate of the Royal Conservatoire of Scotland's BA Acting course.

Recent theatre credits include: *Mr Moonlight, Mooning* (Òran Mór); *Moorcroft* (Tron Theatre); *Is That You, Santa? Maw Goose* (Macrobert Arts Centre); *The Panopticon* (National Theatre of Scotland); *Hel* (Traverse Theatre); *Mother Goose* (Byre Theatre); *Snow White and the Seven Dames* (Perth Theatre). Television and radio credits include: *Traces 2* (Alibi); *Leaving, An Eye for a Killing* (BBC Radio Scotland); *The 5000* (BBC Radio 4); *Questions for Quiz Shows, The Blackwood* (BBC Radio North/Edinburgh Fringe).

CARYS HOBBS (Set & Costume Design)

Carys trained in design at QMU, Edinburgh. Her most recent designs include CATS Award 2022 Best Production winner *Medea* (Bard in the Botanics); *Moorcroft* (Tron Theatre); *Walking Tall Tales* (Tron Theatre Education); *The Dutch Courtesan* (RCS) and *Snow White* (The Byre) in 2022.

Prior to 2020 her credits include *Bingo!* (Stellar Quines and Grid Iron); *Coriolanus Vanishes* (Fire Exit); *Last Tango in Partick* (NTS); CRUDE (with Grid Iron and GlasGlow for Itison). For Tron Theatre she has also designed, *Shall Roger Casement Hang? Colquhoun and MacBryde, Happy Days* and *Brothers Karamazov*.

Carys has been the Head of Design for Bard in the Botanics since 2014 with designs including 2022's *Much Ado About*

Nothing, *Antony and Cleopatra*, *Measure for Measure*, *The Taming of the Shrew*, *Coriolanus*, *Dr Faustus*, *Romeo and Juliet* and *The Merchant of Venice*. Carys leads the Bard in the Botanics placement scheme for in-training costumiers to get professional experience throughout the year.

BAILEY NEWSOME (Mince)

Bailey is from Glasgow and graduated from the BA Acting course at the Royal Conservatoire of Scotland in 2019. Stage credits include: *Write Off* (Òran Mór/Traverse Theatre); *1902* (Saltire Sky); *A Wee Swatch of Oor Wullie, A Potted Christmas Carol, Oor Wullie: The Musical, A-Z of Dundee, Tay Bridge* (Dundee Rep); *San Diego, Humbug! The Breathing House, Strucken Moon, Julius Caesar, Philistines and Middletown* (Royal Conservatoire of Scotland); *Blackout* (Glasgow Acting Academy/NT New Connections).

Television credits include: *Scot Squad; The Sunny* (The Comedy Unit); *The Field of Blood* (BBC Scotland).

JATINDER SINGH RANDHAWA (Mick)

Jatinder Singh Randhawa is an actor from Glasgow who graduated from New College Lanarkshire in 2017. Theatre credits include: *Cinderella the Musical* (Dundee Rep); *Peter Gynt* (National Theatre); *The Arrival, Solar Bear, Cinderella* (all Citizens Theatre) and *Snowflake* (Pleasance Theatre).

Film and television credits include: *Scot Squad* (The Comedy Unit); *The Control Room*; *The Nest* (BBC); *Crime* (ITV); *Shepherd* (Golden Crab); *Courier Culture* (NTS/BBC Scotland).

SANTINO SMITH (Noodles)

Santino Smith trained at the Royal Welsh College of Music and Drama.

Theatre credits include: Eddie Steeples in *Underwood Lane* (Tron Theatre); Noodles in *Moorcroft* (Tron Theatre); Davey in *Jerusalem* (The Watermill); Dax in *The Unemployed Actor's Union*; Brodie in *The Real Thing* (Theatre Royal Bath/Rose Theatre, Kingston).

Television and film credits include: Joao in *Sadie* (BBC4/BBCNI/Lyric Theatre); John in *Lynn + Lucy* (BBC Films).

DYLAN WOOD (Tubs)

Dylan Wood trained at the Bristol Old Vic Theatre School.

His theatre work includes: *Meet Me At The Knob* (Òran Mór); *549: Scots of the Spanish Civil War* (Wonder Fools); *Underwood Lane* (Tron Theatre); *Orphans* (National Theatre of Scotland); *Close Quarters* (Sheffield Theatres); *Teddy* (Watermill Theatre/UK tour); *Electric Eden* (Shanghai Arts Festival/Not Too Tame Theatre Company) and *King Lear* (Bristol Old Vic).

Television work includes: *Dog Days* (BBC); *Unfair* (ALL4); *Sister Boniface* (BBC); *Midsomer Murders* (ITV) and *Casualty* (BBC).

TRON THEATRE

Tron Theatre is a unique and flagship organisation as the West of Scotland's only mid-scale producing venue which delivers challenging new and contemporary performance for the people of Glasgow, Scotland, and worldwide while at the same time playing a vital role at the heart of the Scottish theatre community and facilitating participation in the arts amongst people of all ages, race, ability, and gender.

Recent Tron Theatre Company productions include David Ireland's *Cyprus Avenue*; *La Performance*, a co-production with the International Visual Theatre, Paris; John Byrne's *Underwood Lane*; Eilidh Loan's *Moorcroft*; Gary McNair's adaptation of the Ben Jonson farce, *The Alchemist*; *The Ugly One* by Marius von Mayenberg; Jo Clifford's adaptation of *The Taming of the Shrew*, Enda Walsh's *Ballyturk*; *Ma, Pa and the Little Mouths* by Martin McCormick; Peter Arnott's *Shall Roger Casement Hang?* Martin McDonagh's *The Lonesome West and Isobel McArthur's Pride and Prejudice* (*sort of)*, Tron's co-production with Blood of the Young which had its premiere at the venue in 2018, toured nationally, and opened in the autumn of 2021 at the Criterion Theatre in London's West End, receiving an Olivier Award in 2022 for Best Entertainment or Comedy.

Tron Theatre Company is a supported by Creative Scotland and is a Scottish Registered Charity No: SC012081.

If you would like to make a donation to support the work of Tron Theatre please visit, https://www.tron.co.uk/donate/

www.tron.co.uk

For the Tron Theatre

Artistic Director	**Andy Arnold**
Executive Director	**Patricia Stead**
Finance Manager	**Kate Bell**
Artistic Producer	**Viviane Hullin**
Artistic Producer (maternity cover until May 2023)	**Seona McClintock**
Artist Development Coordinator	**Imogen Stirling**
Creative Learning Manager	**Lisa Keenan**
Creative Learning Officer	**Debbie Montgomery**
Creative Learning Coordinator	**Catherine Ward-Stoddart**
Office Manager	**Lucy Button**
Building Manager	**Iain MacLeod**
Administrator	**Alice Sufferin**
Payroll Officer	**Fiona Wilkie**
Production Manager	**Laura Walshe**
Technical Manager	**Mark Hughes**
Technical Stage Manager	**Jason McQuaide**
Stage Manager	**Suzanne Goldberg**
Venue Technician	**Alex Hatfield**
Venue Technician	**Craig Crawford**
Head of Marketing and Communications	**Lindsay Mitchell**
Marketing and Communications Officer	**Danielle Gray**
Box Office and Front of House Manager	**Khaliq Ahmed**
Duty Managers	**Francesca Rullo**, **Gabriela Cerda** and **Michelle Lynch** (Depute)

Thanks to all of our box office assistants, ushers and cleaners.

NATIONAL THEATRE OF SCOTLAND

National Theatre of Scotland is a Theatre Without Walls. We don't have our own building. Instead, we bring theatre to you. From the biggest stages to the smallest community halls, we showcase Scottish culture at home and around the world. We have performed in airports and tower blocks, submarines and swimming pools, telling stories in ways you have never seen before. We want to bring the joy of theatre to everyone. Since we were founded in 2006, we have produced hundreds of shows and toured all over the world. We strive to amplify the voices that need to be heard, tell the stories that need to be told and take work to wherever audiences are to be found.

Artistic Director & Chief Executive **Jackie Wylie**
Executive Director **Brenna Hobson**
Chair **Jane Spiers**

For the latest information on all our activities, visit us online at www.nationaltheatrescotland.com or follow us on:

Twitter @NTSOnline

Facebook @NationalTheatreScotland

YouTube: @ntsonline

Instagram: @ntsonline

TikTok: @ntsonline

National Theatre of Scotland is core funded by Scottish Government Riaghaltas na h-Alba.

National Theatre of Scotland, a company limited by guarantee and registered in Scotland (SC234270) is a registered Scottish charity (SC033377).

Writer's note

My dad used to take me to watch local teams play when I was a wee girl. By this point he was stood, sulking on the side lines in the rain as his knees were 'getting on'. As I got older, my dad would tell me stories about the teams he played for and other parts of his life. Events that I couldn't begin to imagine living through. I soon realised that joining teams to play the games and win the cups wasn't why these men put all their time and effort into running these clubs in their spare time. It was because these men loved each other. Loved each other to the point we find ourselves in this play. Reliving the past in hope it will change the things that haunt us years later and wishing to right the wrongs. Regardless of events that took place, either from their lack of understanding, or at times, unwillingness to understand, these boys truly loved each other. I haven't known friendship like it.

We are now living in a society where everything is instant, and we are constantly on the go. Taking time to connect with my dad about 'the old days' was so refreshing. He could talk for hours, without his phone buzzing or checking social media feeds. His eyes would light up at the mention of Sooty Bear or if someone started their sentence with 'Mind that time he . . .'

These lads invested time into each other, more so now as they reflect back. It's something I don't think people do enough in this day and age.

You could listen to the stories my dad and his mates tell for hours and never get bored at the sheer volume of interesting and dynamic events which happened in their lives. Now this story is inspired by events from different teams and different stages of my dad's life. He played for many teams, but the name Moorcroft always stuck in my head. I always said, 'That's a cracking name for a play'. This story has been inspired by real stories shared in pubs, interviews, discussions about the world we live in today, documentaries, music and even something as small as someone nickname has given us a full blown character in this play. I wanted to take their stories and push it further, for us, the audience, to learn from the characters' mistakes, laugh at their friendships and normalise their loss in order to see versions of ourselves reflected back to us.

My dad opened up to me about how he truly felt when his mates were going through some incredibly tough times. This broke my heart. Only now, at fifty years old, was he able to let his guard down. This is the result of young boys not allowing themselves to be honest about their emotions because they were persistently told to 'man up' or 'act like a man'. The stigma around men's mental health is still so alarming and is as prevalent today as it was in the 1980s. Mental health is slowly but surely been taken more seriously but we still have a long way to go when it comes to encouraging young men to talk openly and freely about their emotions without feeling shame or judgement. I understand what a huge privilege it was to go to drama school, where talking about emotions and expressing yourself was completely accepted and encouraged. I was also exposed to beautiful people and cultures when moving out of a small town, something these characters never got the chance to experience. When writing *Moorcroft* I wanted to make sure I was portraying the raw, truthful picture of the working-class men I grew up with and giving them the respect they deserve but also reflect the rough parts back to them in order to learn vital lessons we all need to learn.

Theatre can be an extremely intimidating if you haven't had the privilege of going. I speak to friends and relatives who still express this stereotype towards the theatre as 'It's not my thing. I won't understand all that Shakespeare talk. Goes over my head'. There are so many reasons why this stereotype still exists. There isn't enough work done to encourage people from all different backgrounds into the theatre world and when being introduced to theatre, they have never saw something that personally speaks to them. They have never saw themselves reflected back.

My dad and some of the lads the *Moorcroft* characters are based on found it so strange I took such a deep interest in their teenage years that I wanted to make a play based on either something perceived as being so small, like a nickname or an opinion they use to have. They considered their stories to be 'Just the usual'. Typical west of Scotland attitude that we need to stamp out. I was shocked to hear this because as you will see, these characters are unbelievably special, each with vital stories to tell and without the men that inspired me to create them, we wouldn't have *Moorcroft* today.

This is why we need more working-class stories, writers, directors, actors, voices in our industry. We need to give these stories and the people who inspire them power and ownership. I remember being told at drama school that my accent was 'far too Scottish' when reading Lady Macbeth . . . I mean . . . really? We are still condoning this stereotype that theatre has a certain type of voice and that, that voice should be front and centre on stage.

Moorcroft is set in a working-class town in the late 1980s where there wasn't enough encouragement for people to seek more opportunities beyond the small town. To be completely honest, not much has changed. Small towns around Scotland can still be very close minded. Their views on the world are dated and having any sort of political motivated conversation in the pub turns into a kicking and screaming match. Hence why they don't have them. No one can be rational.

Some of the issues raised in the play are close to home for a lot of people. Some of the issues you might have never gone through and never will, but I urge you to think about the different journeys *Moorcroft* explores when you are on your trip home. Especially the ones you have never been on. It's important we learn and grow from other people's honesty and believe me, these characters are honest.

We were extremely lucky to have original items of clothing from the boys. Sooty's famous parka jacket he gave to my dad, was given to us. These pieces of clothing are so special as they have been worn making memories by the boys themselves in real life and by our actors in rehearsal rooms.

Now, we share these memories with you. I love these characters and this story. Even though there are moments that make my heart hurt, I am proud of these boys. I am grateful for the lessons these characters have taught me. I know more about who I am because of what these boys went through, and I hope they have the same effect on you. They are incredibly brave and incredibly powerful, and this play is for them.

I dedicate this play to my dad, Garry Loan, all his friends and the families these characters are based on. Every single one of you is so strong and I hope we bring lessons and laughter to everyone who watches us play. A huge thank you to everyone who has been involved with the making of *Moorcroft* and special thank you to Carl Prekopp and David Pugh who saw the importance of this story from day one and to Andy Arnold who has been an incredibly important member of the Moorcroft family. Grab your scarves. It's nearly kick off. MON THE CROFT!

Eilidh

Notes

The movement in this play shouldn't feel disjointed. Football is a dance. It's a routine. It's rehearsed. The actors must support each other and stay fixated on the mimed ball as no football should be used as a prop during this play.

Garry

Garry is fifty years old. When he is addressing the audience, we are in the present day. We watch an older man trying to relive his youth as he embodies himself at the age of nineteen. His vocal quality should become younger as well as his physically as he loses himself in the past. The rest of the cast remain the age they are cast.

Moorcroft

Dedicated to **Garry Loan**

Pre-match

Present day. Scotland. The set is many places (pitch, pub, nightclub etc.).

Upstage left stands an old Scottish pub (on wheels as it moves around through the show). Two old school P.E. benches sit either side of the playing space.

A rope washing line runs across the stage. A 50th birthday balloon in the middle.

Garry *exits the pub. Lights a cigarette. He looks to the balloon.*

He pops the balloon with his cigarette. He looks out to the audience.

Garry   Shat it!

Beat.

Fifty. Christ sake. Who needs balloons at fuckin fifty? I thought I'd be a retired fitbawller livin in a beach hoose in fuckin Spain by this point . . . didn't we all.

But . . . naw . . . still grafting away . . . thinking 'How the fuck um I fuckin fifty?'

He speeeds up.

I canny wait till I'm auld. Ancient. When ye can walk doon the street talkin to yurself and calling people arseholes and everybody goes 'Awwwk, it's fine, look he's a wee auld man'.

Canny do that at fifty, might still get a doin.

He takes a draw.

I suppose we should start really. I mean . . . reason ye came oot the night wisny fur my birthday, now wis it?

What I will say before kick aff is . . . This is a real story, right. Blood, guts, funerals the lot. I'll tell it with nae filter.

It isn't . . . all . . . ye know . . . mad bits of furniture whoshhhin' in from the sky. We do not come oot in fancy sparkly costumes singing la-de-da and we all live fuckin happily ever after. Naw. You've been warned fae the start.

He looks around. A moment then back to the audience, he gets real.

The thing is . . . we lived a life where everything was so boring and shite, ye couldny be arsed brushin yur teeth some mornings.

Working the same shitty jobs, sittin in the same shitty pub, on the same shitty stool, drinking the same shitty lager, doing the same shitty thing. Day in day oot.

But we were just dain wit we thought was right.

He backtracks . . .

A team. A team of wit? A team of players? A bunch of mates comin the gither to huv a kick aboot? Wits new?

Folk wid ask us, wit the fuck I was tryin tae dae when I started it aw. 'Stick to wit ye know, Garry.'

He puffs his chest and is ready. Pops the rest of the balloons.

But fuck that! It's the late 1980s. I'm nowhere near fifty. I'm a young good lookin nineteen-year-auld, with a heavy heart but a right fire in my belly . . . I'm fuckin sick of sticking tae wit I know.

We begin. A whistle. We roll back.

'Love Will Tear Us Apart' by Joy Division mixed with the sounds of the 1980s. News headlines, radio shows, TV presenters, Maggie Thatcher talking, riots, sounds of the working-class town, cars, shop bells, pints being poured, Scottish football pundits.

Boom. Six boys enter as time rolls back. We see a montage of working-class life. Getting ready for the day. They all exit and **Tubs** *remains with his bucket and brush.*

Scene 1

TUBS

Tubs *stands on the bar, painting over a new poster. He turns down the radio on the wall. 'Love Will Tear Us Apart' fades. A sandwich wrapped in tin foil sits on the bar.*

Tubs   Spit it oot, Garry. I've goat fifteen miutes to get this up.

Garry   Wit is that yur adverting?

Tubs   Washing powder.

Garry   Oh right, wit one?

Tubs   Why do you gee a fuck?

Garry   My maw uses one and it itches . . .

Tubs   I don't have time for this, Gaz.

Garry   Right . . . so, I wis walkin hame fae my work and I stoaped tae watch the wee lads in Robbie Park.

Tubs   Pedo bastard.

Garry   Naw, no lit that. Like just their fitbaw and they were pure good wee guys and I thought fuck sake that use tae be us lot.

Tubs   Aye, when we were ten, Garry.

Garry   What if we, us, the lads set up a team. A wee six a side team.

Tubs   Where dae you pull these ideas fae?

Garry   Come oan, it would be class us all together oan the pitch again. Keepin fit and healthy

Tubs   Fit and healthy, look at ye . . .

Garry   and . . . well . . . seeing each other.

Look at aw the lassies fae school, right. Going fur fuckin 'afternoon drinks' or 'a girls' night at Lizzy's' and we take the piss but at least they aw still fuckin see each other.

Tubs   Aye. True . . . you've goat a point.

Garry   We can enter a wee league and that.

Tubs   You mean play against actual other real teams?

Garry   Well, that is how fitbaw works, is it not?

Tubs   Tournaments? Wit for six a side fitbaw? HA HA.

Garry   They do do them.

Tubs   Is that right, aye? Well . . . we will be shite. Pure utter garbage, mate. Laughed at, if ye will. 'Look at those auld fuddys tryin tae make a fitbaw team.' 'Aye look at those fuckin dobbers.' 'Wit a bunch a auld fannies'.

Garry   We are hardly fuckin auld, Tubs.

Tubs   Mate. A whole nineteen years we've been oan this earth. I'm auld. Your auld.

Garry   Wit the fuck is wrang wae you? Tubs. Come on, man. It's not lit professional fitbaw. It's a bit of fun.

Tubs   I'm too auld for fun, Gaz.

Garry   I'm fucking bored oot my tits in this place, fuck sake. Mate. Come on /

Tubs   Come on?

Garry *turns to audience.* **Tubs** *begins to move in slow motion. The past, memories, slowly floating. Slow motion as* **Garry** *leaves the past for a second.*

Garry   Tubs. Called Tubs because his surname was Tubard, nothing tae dae with him being actually fat or that . . . look at the guy, legs like a sparra. Tubard like me . . . a skint bastard, at least he still had a joab dain the buildboards. But he'd eat shite for 50p.

So . . . When I flash this in front of his face, watch as the coin disappears, and I bag myself the next best defender since Danny McGrain . . . ohhhh controversial among the old blues there . . . Oh Tubs.

They snap back to the scene. **Garry** *flashes 50p.*

Tubs   / Aye. Aye aright. Aye. Only if you're in goals.

Garry *flings him a coin.*

Scene 2

SOOTY

Sooty *enters dressed in his parka jacket and freshly pressed Fred Perry polo shirt. The pride in his clothes. Ginger hair cut and styled to mod perfection.*

Sooty   Ya bastard.

Tubs   Ohh parka boy.

Sooty   A fitbaw team?

Garry   How no?

Sooty   Wit age are you? Five?

Tubs   See, telt ye. Laughed at.

Garry   Naw. 'Cause there's fuck aw else tae dae and takes yur mind aff how shit it is.

Sooty   And you think a wee fitbaw team will solve aw that, Gazza, aye?

Garry   Fuck off, Sooty! The team. It's a bit of fun.

Tubs *sits and eats his tin foil wrapped sandwich.*

Tubs   Aye come on, Phil Daniels, 'We are the mods, we are the mods'.

Sooty   Fuck up, Freddie Mercury. You don't even know wit a mod is.

Tubs   A mod . . . (*Clears his throat.*) By definition. Is a big fanny like you, who walks aboot in fuckin Fred fuckin Perry's big green jaickets, listening tae The Konks /

Sooty   / The Kinks.

Tubs   Aye. Them. Shite. Driving aboot on yur pathetic excuse fur a motorbike tryin tae look cool as fuck when really everybody thinks you look like an absolute dobber.

Garry *to audience.* **Sooty** *and* **Tubs** *slow motion.* **Tubs** *slaps* **Sooty** *over the head with paint brush, messing his hair.*

Garry   Sooty. Ginger. Mod. Guy fuckin loved his clothes right. Always in that parka, man. No matter the season. He was mad into the scene. If he could shag his moped he would have. Never leaves the hoose without that hair been absolutely perfect. Brilliant guy and a fuckin brilliant player but it would take mare than a shiny coin to bribe him.

The scene snaps back.

Tubs (*continuing*)   We are the mods . . .

Sooty   Fuck up you. (*He fixes hair with comb.*)

Garry   Right. Enough. Sooty . . . The Small Faces record to join the team.

Sooty   Wit? Your Small Faces one? The one you've goat all proper . . . it's been signed, and in the case and that?

Garry   Aye. Sooty.

Sooty   But you love that, I couldn't take it /

Garry   / Record for the team.

Sooty   Aye. I'm in, Gazza.

Tubs   Seriously? I got a fuckin 50p?

Sooty   Ha ha, get it right up ye!

Tubs   Wrap it. C'mere.

They chase each other off. **Sooty** *steals* **Tubs'** *sandwich.*

Scene 3

MICK AND PAUL

Mick *and* **Paul** *enter.* **Mick** *in his work waistcoat – finishing off* **Paul***'s haircut with comb and barber's coat.*

Paul   Brilliant idea, Garry boy.

Garry   Aye, I'm glad ye think so Paul, mate. We just need the kits, money fur the pitches and aw that stuff.

Paul   We could dae race nights and that.

Garry *to audience.* **Mick** *and* **Paul** *slow motion.*

Garry   Paul. Pure dead popular. Well . . . until he goat us aw suspended for setting stink bombs aff in the assembly hall. Paul is that bawbag that will drink hof a pint and start a fight with his ain reflection . . . Oh here . . . remember I said that . . . I'll come back to that.

Snap back to the scene.

Paul   I'm in, Gaz. Canny wait to get playin again, eh Mick?

Mick   Naw, naw, naw. You know I don't play anymore, Garry . . .

Garry *to audience.* **Mick** *and* **Paul** *slow motion.*

Garry   Mick. He wis gonna play professional fitbaw right. I'm talkin he wis getting scouted for every bloody team. Under 18s. He wis gettin tae leave school for the try oots and that. We all knew, Mick, wan day he would make the first team but . . .

Snap back to scene.

Paul   Aw mon, Mick, mate. You were the best.

Mick   Were. Not noo.

Garry   You could still take the pish oot us aw.

Mick   Maybe three year ago.

Garry   It's hardly a fuckin long time ago, Mick. Look mate, we are aw in the same boat, mate. Aw unfit. Out of shape. Look at that fat cunt.

He points to **Paul** *who is shaping his hair in the mirror – thinking he is beautiful.*

Paul   Fat my arse.

Garry   Aye, Paul. It is . . .

Mick *laughs.*

Paul   Cheeky bastard . . . Well, best dig the auld trainers oot then . . .

Paul *exits.* **Garry** *slaps his arse.*

Garry   Soon as we get trainin and that. Get oor fitness up. It will be brilliant, Mick? Be good tae see ye back oan that park again, eh?

Mick   Best of luck wae it, Gaz.

He exits. **Garry** *to the audience.*

Garry   Me and wee Mick met when we were kids. Our maws use tae work doon the wool shop the gither and when it wis the summer holidays we use tae go doon and help them.

There was wan time. Must have been ten year auld. Some auld buddy took a tumble ootside the shop and my maw and Mick's maw run oot to help. So we hud tae run the shop oor self. Thing is aboot this wool shop wis, they hud dead funny names fur the colours. 'Sunrise Yellow' and 'Midnight Blue' and aw that shite. So me and Mick decided tae go round the whole shop and change aw the wee tags. So ye hud like orange wool called 'Army Green'. That's two colours ye do not want tae mix up in Glasgow. It took oor maws three hoors tae go roon and change them back. Goat grounded fur two weeks after that.

We never helped that much in the shop as we got aulder, fitbaw took the priority oan the weekends, but I remember wan Saturday, me and my maw were away visiting my auntie over in East Kilbride. Mick and his maw were in the shop themselves and some fuckin nutter came in and glassed Mick's maw. Over the heed. We rushed back and met her in the hospital and that, police asked if this wis a wan aff, could we remember any 'suspicious behaviour', bla fucking bla. Was it hell a wan aff. Mick and his wee maw goat it aw the time in the shop. And ootside the shop. Bottles thrown at the hoose. Shite posted through the letter boax. Mick goat called aw sorts fae other lads at school or fae other teams we played wie.

Then ye see him oan that fitbaw park. He wis fucking unreal. Next thing ye know . . . slowly . . . the other teams stopped wie the name calling and the fights became over him, not wie him. Fitbaw wis the wan thing Mick won at . . . Until he goat injured.

He hud tae sit the season oot, wan season, after he wis better . . . nae team wanted him. Career over. Goodbye. Never stepped back oan a fitbaw park again. Too raw fur him I suppose. Goat a job in the barber's and that wis that.

Garry *moves on.*

Garry   So . . . who else did we huv? Oh Christ . . . aye . . . him . . . This is . . . eh . . . This is Mince, he's called Mince because. Awwk you'll find oot.

Scene 4

BACK TOGETHER

The pub spins and transforms into the changing rooms. **Sooty**, **Noodles**, **Paul** *all stand getting ready. Dressed in old tops and sports wear.* **Noodles** *is changing out a shirt.* **Mince** *enters doing frog jumps trying to pass it off as warming up. He then takes a deep lunge in front of* **Paul**.

Paul   Mince, stoap that, I can see wit ye hud fur yur fuckin breakfast.

Mince   Here, Noodles . . . Wit is it ye dae in those offices again?

Noodles   Claims investigation. Borin.

Mince   Borin? Investigatin? Is that no wit the police dae?

Investigate stuff? Pure Sherlock Holmes over here?

Paul   Shut up, Froggy Mcgee.

Mince   I wasn't talkin to you, Paul.

Noodles   I basically decide who gets money and who dosny. So, if someone is claiming money fur an injury in an accident and then I spot them . . . playing fitball, for example. They get done.

Mince   So . . . I wis fuckin right? Sherlock fuckin Holmes, Paul, ya tottie.

Paul   'Pure fuckin Sherlock.' It's the way ye say things. Thick as Mince. Ha! I'm glad people huvny stoapped callin you that.

Sooty   Aye. Fuckin hilarious!

Mince   Naw. It's no. I hate it. My nana hates it mare. She goes tae me 'Imagine me telling your wains wit yur nickname wis at school.'

Paul   Wit wains? Your no huvin wains.

Mince   Why?

Noodles   'Cause you canny tell the difference between holes.

Laugh.

Paul   Mine is a shiter, int it. 'Oh wit's your name?' Paul. Right. You're just gettin calt Paul.

Noodles   Noodles? A mean, wit even is that?

Paul   We thought curly pubies looked like noodles.

Sooty   It's a belter.

Garry *to audience. Lads slow motion.*

Garry   Smart lad, Noodles. Lucky tae still huv work comin in giving the circumstances and that. But he's no like the rest of us. It's a big office job. Never let oan how clever he wis. Only wan that stayed oan at school and that. Of course, we take the piss oot the clever cunt.

Snap back into scene.

Noodles   Pure shite.

Mick *enters at the back and watches the boys. They don't notice him.*

Sooty   'Wits yur pals name. He's pure nice so he is.' 'Aw this is Noodles.'

Paul   'Noodles? Is that really his name?'

Sooty   'Oh Aye!'

Paul   'Oooo and why dae ye get calt that?'

Sooty   'Pull doon his troosers, darlin, and ye might fun oot.'

Mick   Aye, she'd pull them doon and be disappointed.

The other boys look and laugh.

Sooty   Mick, mate? You . . . you playin, aye?

Mick   Well . . . I'm ready to get kicking the arse oot of you lot fur striker.

Noodles   Thank fuck we've goat ye, Mick. Even this dafty hus made the team.

Mince   What?

Paul   Aww, ye heard that over there, did ye Sherlock?

Mince   Fuck up.

Sooty   Here it's gone hof past . . . where the fuck is Garry . . .

The boys slow.

Beat. **Garry** *pauses he has got completely lost in watching his friends. Breaking into the scene again.*

Garry   Oh shite! Sorry I was just enjoying myself there . . .

Hello, ladies.

The boys snap back to full speed.

Chorus   Here he fucking is. Aboot time, mate. Fuckin wit time dae ye call this? Late prick.

Mince   Aye, you're late, ya pick.

They all look at him as if 'too far mate'.

Garry   Well, so . . . cheers fue comin. Even you, Mick. You aw made it. You aw know why we are here.

Noodles   Starting a boy band.

Mince   Aye, like Duran Duran (*Pronounces it wrong.*)

Noodles   It's Duran Duran.

Garry   Seriously boys. Wits the harm in us gettin the gither again and kickin a baw about. We can only be dain good fur ourselves. Keepin fit /

Paul   aye aye, get oan wae it.

Garry   Right. First order of business. Money, Tubs will be late tonight because he wis goin roon stickin these up.

He holds up a shitty homemade flyer and begins passing them around. Spelt wrong.

Mince   Look at them! Stunning. Beautiful. Best flyer I have seen in my puff.

Noodles   I wonder, who made these.

Mince   Aye, yours truly.

Paul   Naw.

Mince   Yes. Paul, I did /

Paul   / NAW. Look at that.

Sooty   Aw fucking hell, that's a sin, man. Huv ye handed these oot, Garry?

Garry   Well, Tubs hus been aye, think he wis dain the other pubs oan his way hame fae work?

Mick   It says fundraising raffel.

Garry   Naw, it's a raffle.

Noodles   Aye, but this says raffel.

They all look at **Mince**.

Mince   I thought that's how you spelt it.

Mick   You are a fuckin plonker.

Paul   Aye well in, Mince, ya daft prick.

Garry   It says fundraising, so everyone knows wit that is. It's oan Saturday at the community centre. Music, my maw's dain food.

(*Wolf whistle.*)

Mick   Oy Oy.

Paul   Need a hand butterin those sandwiches, Mags darlin?

Garry   Drap it.

The others giggle.

Garry   We will huv the 'raffle'. Bit of dancin, roll in a bit of cash fur us tae get money tae book the pitches. After that, money fur oor kits.

Noodles   I could dae those mad fitbaw cards roon the office.

Garry   Belter, Noodles. Great, mate. Bleed those posh cunts dry. But we all need to work hard, right?

Sooty   But wit if we are shite?

Paul   Aye, I'm no goin oan a park and losin. I fucking hate losin.

Sooty   Aye Paul, we know. Treated P.E. like the bloody World Cup.

Garry   We aw just need tae make a fuckin go at this. Right, boys?

Mince (*with passion and loud*)   AYE!

The rest look at him. What a dick.

Garry   See! That's the passion we're lookin fur. So let's start easy. Wee jog up the park. GO.

The jog movement begins.

Noodles   I'm gonna say right now. I've goat a sare ankle.

Sooty   Aye and I've goat a sare chest.

All the boys 'Awww' sarcastically.

Sooty   Shut it. Think it's an infection or somethin.

Mince   Aw here, my nana hud that last week. Chest infection. She goat given that mad class painkiller fur it. Swiped a strip when I wis up seein her oan Sunday if ye want me tae get ye some.

They stop jogging to look at **Mince**. **Mince** *continues to jog.*

Noodles   You took your nana's painkillers?

Mick   You sad bastard.

Mince *stops jogging.*

Mince   Aye, no fur me tae take them or anythin like that. It's just 'cause in the future when the world hus an apocalypse, I've goat another medicine in my 'personal emergency stash'.

Paul   Wit the actual fuck are you, Mince?

Mince   A fitbaw player now, lads.

He overlaps the boys.

Noodles (*calling over*)   Gaz? We goat a name yit?

Garry   Ehhh naw, wit yous think?

Sooty   Big Dicks FC.

Paul   Shaggers United.

Mince   Suck Oor Hairy Big Massive Huge Big Cocks City?

Silence.

Sooty   Well, that's a shiter.

Tubs *enters. Covered in mud. They stop running.*

Mick   Ahh! Look at this tadger! Wit the fuck happened tae you?

Tubs   That auld Moorcroft field is gettin dug up. Apparently, they are turnin it into new fitbaw pitches, I thought 'Oh perfect I better check this out' and I scuddied it oan my arse.

Paul   No cunt runs through that Moorcroft field, it's a pure bog.

Tubs   Not fur long. New pitches.

Garry   New pitches, boys? New team!

Mick   Moorcroft? That's somethin that'll get folk chanting.

They all look.

Garry   Moorcroft?

Noodles   Mon the Croft.

Scene 5

TRAINING

'Blue Monday' by New Order builds as the boys begin training.
Working through different drills. They glide and run and sprint.

Garry *to audience.*

Garry   We trained every Tuesday. It wis class. The boys
being the gither again. Gettin oor bodies aw healthy again.
We were feeling oor age. Youthfulness instead of auld
duffers. Dain somethin that wisny just work and mare work.

Back to the lads.

Garry   Right, boys. Up the top. Get that blood pumping.
That heart jumping. First time since P.E.

That is it, boys . . . Loosen those hips. Just like yur nan
taught me, Mince.

The boys move into motion. The improve in speed as **Garry***'s speech*
continues.

Garry   It felt like the start of somethin. Somethin fuckin
achievable and it felt . . .

FUCKING BRILLIANT!

He jumps back in to training.

All   Mon the fuckin Croft.

Training ends and the changing room swings back to the pub. 'Blue Monday' fades into the pub radio.

Scene 6

PINK

The boys sit in the pub. Muttering as **Paul** *and* **Mince** *carry the drinks over. They sit.*

Noodles *enters with the kit bag. He has his sunglasses and a Rangers scarf on. He is like a famous gangster.*

Mince   Mammy, Daddy pass me mine first.

Paul   Mince. Shut up and sit doon.

Mince   I'm just excited.

Paul   Oh aye, like it's Christmas, aye. Sit doon, ya dafty.

Noodles   Dae ye want it, but?

Chorus   Aye!

Noodles   But dae ye want it?

Chorus   Aye / Hurry up ya bastard / Move it / Mon ya prick.

Noodles   I said, dae ye want it!!!!

They all cheer and he drops the kit bag down the middle of the pub.

Noodles   Right hud yur horses. Before ye aw clamber in tae get yur taps . . . (*Clears his throat.*) I would like to thank everyone fur aw their hard work raising money fur oor first kit, however because of me takin the fitbaw cards into my work and . . .

Tubs   Posh prick . . .

Noodles (*ignoring him*)   AND rising all the money while you lazy bastards sat aroond dain fuck aw /

Mince (*interrupting*)   Ehh, naw. Naw, that's no true. I goat us two quid.

Noodles   Two quid. Everyone, Mince . . . raised . . . £2, gee him a round of applause.

Mince *thinks this is genuine.*

Noodles   That £2 got us . . . this.

He takes his middle finger out his pocket.

Mince   Naw, it wis tae go towards the kits.

Noodles   It was two quid, Mince.

Mince   Arsehole. I worked hard fur that.

Sooty   HA! Dain wit? You're a dozy bastard.

Mince (*hesitant*)   Eh . . . dosny matter.

Garry   Naw, c'mon, Mince, oot wie it now.

Mick   Wit did ye dae? You know the rules.

Tubs   Nae secrets.

Mince   Nothing.

Garry   Spit it oot!

Noodles   Get it telt!

They all pressure him.

Chorus   Tell it. Tell it. Tell it. TELL IT.

Mince   Right, FINE! Fuck sake . . .

He takes a beat.

I cleaned my nana's teeth . . . aright.

Sooty   Ya wit . . .

Mince   A cleaned my nana's teeth and she geed me a few coins.

Garry Why the fuck . . . was you cleaning yur nana's teeth?

Mince I told ye, she's goat a sare chest and that so she couldny get up tae the sink and that so she said, 'Son, I'll gee you a few coins if ye dae ma teeth fur me.'

Mick That's no right, mate.

Noodles Na the worst thing is, sad bastard took cash aff her fur that.

Sooty Well, if she couldn't get tae the sink fur her teeth, wit did she dae fir the toilet then, Mince?

Tubs Where dae ye think that tenner came fae to buy this round?

They erupt.

Mince Right, fuck off, ha bloody ha. Get these kits oot. I'm gagging to see them.

Noodles Well, I have managed tae get us oor very own kits. So basically, without me . . . and nanny fangs over there, we would be playin oor first match oan Saturday in oor auld P.E. kits. So, you can aw kiss oor ass.

Paul Aye, aye, smart arse, fucking hurry up and get them oot.

Tubs Aye moan, I'm buzzin.

Noodles In 3 . . . 2 . . .1 . . . Right . . . Drumroll please.

They all bang a drum roll as **Noodles** *opens the bag and pulls out a top. The bright pink football top.*

Silence.

Mince Pink.

Pause.

The boys think it's a joke. They laugh.

Paul That's a belter. Get the real wans oot.

Paul *looks through the bag but more pink shirts.*

Christ sake. Right, where are they?

Silence.

Paul   Noodles?

Noodles   Eh . . . that is them.

Paul   Wit?

Beat.

Noodles   I said maroon oan the phone.

They begin to see this is not a joke.

Paul   Maroon? Maroon?

Mince   Wit is a maroon?

Noodles   It's fine. It's just the light. It's no that bad.

Paul   Naw, naw. No that bad? They are fuckin pink shirts, mate.

Tubs   Wits the problem? It's only a pink shirt.

Noodles   Exactly.

Paul   Wit? They are fuckin gay, mate! Drumchappel are gonny lap this right up, in't they. 'Fuckin gay boys.'

Tubs   Calm doon, Paul, it's only a bloody colour. Wit, 'cause they are pink ye think they are 'gay'?

Paul   Aw come aff it, Tubs. Don't say it 'gay' like that. Look at the state a this shite.

He grabs the shirt from **Noodles**.

Tubs   Aw sorry, I didn't realise we were still at fuckin primary school. Wit fuckin age are you lot? It's the fuckin eighties, by Christ. Wearing the colour pink, dosny automatically makes you a 'gay' trust me . . .

Paul (*obviously irritated*)   I'm not playin in no gay shirt, Garry.

Garry *looks to* **Tubs**.

Tubs   Are you for real, Paul?

Paul   Too fuckin right!

Paul *shoves the shirt back into the bag.*

Tubs   Can I ask you something? Just purely oot of curiously, right? You won't play with a gay pink shirt, right? What aboot . . . a gay player?

Paul   Talk shite. Gay folk don't play fitbaw.

Tubs   How?

Paul   'Cause they don't.

Tubs   'Cause they don't.' That is yur only answer, Paul. 'Cause they don't /

Paul   Gay folk don't play fitbaw 'cause they are big poofy, AIDS ridden cunts who walk aboot flailin their arms, singin and screamin, scared tae mess up their hair or get fuckin muddy. They are fuckin arrogant arseholes. The lot of them. Fitbaw is everythin BUT that, Tubs! It's a man's game. Made fur real men. No wee poofy, dick suckin fake wans. So there ye go, mate. Question answered. GAY FOLK DO NOT PLAY FITBAW. Full stoap.

The boys laugh at **Paul** *doing one of his 'bits', an offensive stereotype.*

Tubs   Gay folk aren't real men?

Paul   I've just said that have a no?

Tubs   You mean every word of that, aye? AIDS ridden cunt anaw?

Paul   Do you no listen tae the news, Tubs naw? It's only them fuckers that's goat it.

Paul *drinks his pint. No one else says a thing.*

Tubs   I'm gay.

Paul   Ah right, very good, Tubs is gay, watch yur pint, boys, don't want to get it mixed up with . . .

Tubs   Paul, shut up. SHUT UP.

Silence. **Tubs** *calms himself. He has control of the room. What has slipped out, now must have ownership.*

I am gay. Right. We are no in school anymare . . . I canny fuckin go oan like this. See, because of cunts like you, I've spent my whole teenage life feelin like I canny breath and I'm fuckin sick of it.

'Men should be real men?' OK, but what the fuck is a real man anyways, eh? Enlighten me, Paul?

Talking about fitbaw, and women, and tits. Who shagged who and who can drink mare pints, aye? Is that it?

I refuse tae live the rest of my fuckin life pretendin tae be somethin I'm no when things are finally fuckin changin in the world. Open your fuckin eyes. People are just fuckin people.

Beat.

You got anythin tae say fur yourself mate? Paul?

Paul *sits in silence. Staring at the floor like a child.*

Tubs   Anyone else? Hm . . .?

The boys look away from him. He turns to the pub.

Hus anyone else goat anythin tae fuckin say aboot it? Aboot huving a wee fuckin 'poof' oan the team? Naw?

No one responds.

I'll be playing on Saturday no matter what colour the fuckin strips are.

I'll see you all at training.

He exits. Silence.

Paul   Somebody can change the fuckin subject.

He downs his pint.

Beat.

Mince   I've goat a belter of a skelf oan ma left foot. I wis just walkin in my hoose, and we've goat new floorin doon and I was in my bare feet and I was just walking and I went 'Och . . .'

Paul *slams down his pint.*

Mince   Wit? He said change the fuckin subject.

Garry *to audience.*

Garry   Thing aboot a small toon is. People always want tae change the subject. And . . . we aw knew aboot Tubs. There were several things we all knew aboot but naebody would ever mention it. Because . . . truth is . . . we were fuckin cowards. Scared. Would we fuck talk aboot anything like that?

To be honest and hear me oot, right . . . but . . . it wasn't Paul's fault either. He didn't actually believe any of the stuff he said. None of us did, aboot gay folk or religion or race or that. It's just small-minded shite, stuff we heard from other boys or oor das or grandas in the pub or the bookies and we would say it just tae feel . . . I dunno . . . I'm no standin here excusing it.

Tubs knew the fucking consequences he faced after he stood in that pub that day. This is working-class Scotland folks. Dae ye think people take kindly tae news like his? Dae they fuck.

'You Think You're a Man' by Divine plays.

Tubs *enters in his pink strip. Proud but still holding fear. He begins to dance. Each move links into a punch/kick to himself.*

At the back of the stage, silhouettes of men in the club. Eighties ballroom NYC syle dancing. Layers being removed, as **Tubs** *takes a hit to the floor.*

The stage lights up to reveal the rest of the team in their pink strips, jogging towards **Tubs**. **Tubs** *looks to* **Paul** *next to him. He nods but they say nothing.*

They begin to warm up for the match. **Tubs** *with tears in his eyes. The lads may not understand but they accept. The pub moves into the changing rooms again.*

Scene 7

COUGH

All cast jog into the changing room.

Garry   Right, today's team sheet. Sooty, Tubs, Paul, Mick, Noodles and me. Mince, mate. You're on the bench, buddy.

Mince   Shite.

Chorus   Wehyy. Get it up ye. Ha ha, Mince.

Garry   OK, so, this is it boys. We huv worked oor arses aff to start smashin matches. Like I said, let's no be fannies and fuck it up. You, don't hog the baw. You, don't bloody push people oot the way. And you fuckin run when I tell ye tae run.

Sooty, mate, ye awrite?

Sooty *nods.*

Garry (*continuing*)   Right boys, move your arses. Let's dae this.

They all start to walk out. **Sooty** *is still coughing.* **Garry** *lingers behind.*

Garry   Hurry up, weezy, get that fuckin chest sorted.

Sooty   It's just a wee cold, mate.

Garry   Aye well. Get it seen tae.

Sooty   Wit are you, ma maw?

Garry *turns to the audience.*

Garry   This is the point I wish I could stop because . . .

Scene 8

OOT OOT PLANS

The lads enter again.

Noodles   YES, MY BOYS.

Mick   Two–nil on our first match isn't half bad.

Noodles   Looks like a pint oan me, boys.

Tubs   I'll get the nuts.

Mince   Course you will, you bent bastard.

They all wait for his response. He acts pissed off but he flips into banter.

Tubs   Aye, but I'm your bent bastard.

Noodles   Here, boys. Should we go oot, oot tonight. Lit proper oot. Celebrate in style.

Mince   Savoy then?

Garry   Wit, like a proper clubbin, aye?

Noodles   Fuckin hell. Wit age are you, Garry?

Tubs   I'm up fur it. We've no been up the toon the gither since high school.

Paul   Aye, but no Savoy.

Mince   Wit! Why no Savoy?

Paul   It's shite.

Mince   Savoy's no shite.

Noodles   The dancefloor is carpeted, Mince . . . it's shite.

Mince   Class tunes, but. They dae this mad ABBA mega mix at the end.

Mick   An ABBA mega mix . . .

Mince   Aye, like when all the greatest songs come the gither in wan fusion of sound like . . . 'Waterloo de dee deed um de deed um de dum' into 'The winner take it awwww'

He holds the 'aww' a wee bit too long.

Pause.

Mince   THE WINNER TAKES IT . . .

Chorus   Right! Right, enough, fuck sake, Mince.

Paul   We know wit a fucking mega mix is but fucking ABBA? Savoy is full of gays. Naw.

Mick   Paul!!!

Paul *looks to* **Tubs** *and pats him on the back.*

Paul   Aye, but Tubs isny like wan of those gays that touches yur arse every second and that.

Tubs   Fuckin hell. Wit makes you think any of 'those gays' would want tae even touch your arse, ya ugly cunt!

Mince   Here, Mick, any chance of a quick trim before we head oot?

Chorus   Oh aye. Go on, Mick, Just the sides, or the top.

Mick   Fuck right off. Spendin my night cuttin yur hair.

Tubs   Wit? You did Sooty the other day.

Mick   Aye, he had an appointment.

The lads mock 'Ohh, an appointment'.

Tubs   Aye, ye need four appointments to dae his hair right . . .

Sooty *doesn't respond.*

Garry   Somebody is awfy quiet. You aright, Sooty Bear?

Mick   Aye, course he is, two fuckin goals he set up today.

Noodles   Right mon, let the wain have his mega mix?

Mince   YAS!

Chorus   Mon the fucking Croft.

Scene 9

CLUBBIN

'Male Stripper' by Man 2 Man plays. We see a montage of the getting ready process. The boys in their own homes. Lights appear giving us an insight into what they do on their own. Dancing in the mirror like no one is watching.

The bus ride. (The truck in which the pub and changing room now travels through the space as a bus.) The pissing in the street. The waiting in the nightclub line. Drug taking. The ID for the bouncer. **Mick** *is the only one to get stopped and searched.*

They all enter the club. Music blasting. Their eyes light up. Their dancing styles. They form a boy band – they are in sync, usual pick up routine.

Scene 9.1

BIRDS

All dialogue under club music.

Paul   She's pure lookin at you, mate.

Mince   Naw, she's no.

Mick   Aye, Mince. She is!

Paul   Go over and gee her wan, mate.

Mince *dances to the side of the stage, the boys laugh as he comes back soaking wet, the music heats up. The boys start to come up.* **Sooty** *can't cope. The noise is punching him and the boys' faces twist. He needs to escape. Music bumping in the distance. The pub begins to move around the space fast. Turning and twisting. We end up in the toilets. All exit except* **Garry** *and* **Sooty**.

Scene 10

CANCER

Garry *enters the toilet.* **Sooty** *is vomiting. He wipes his face. Thoughts pour.*

Sooty   3–6, 3–6, 3–6, 3–6 /

Garry   Sooty, mate? You eh . . .

Sooty   An average of 3 to 6 they said. Three to 6. I can't stop the numbers going round in my heed, it's like a broken record. Three to 6. 3 to 6. 3 to 6.

I wrote out a list because she said it would help. The woman that works up the café, gives ye the free chocolate because she feels bad for ye.

Garry   Wit dae ye mean, mate?

Sooty   List all the thing ye want tae achieve, Garry.

I have three things. There is a whole world of achievable things and I can only think of three fuckin things. So.

Tell my family and friends – All my family and friends I love them.

Ride to Brighton like they do in *Quadrophenia*. Be a proper mod.

Win a wee tournament cup with the lads.

I sit and think aboot this list. I can realistically achieve wan thing oan it. I can only tell ma family and friends I love them. But the thing is, I canny even dae that. Because I . . . I don't know wit tae fuckin say. 'Lads. Thanks for being my best pals. Through everythin the gither. I love you'? Naw. We don't . . . say . . .

(*He quickens.*) And I won't see Brighton and I won't lift the cup. Because if I canny go tae Brighton oan my ain scooter, I don't want tae and if I can't lift a wee fucking cup oan my own I don't want tae dae that either. I don't want a fucking charity case tae finish ma list fur me. Some wee bus to come pick me up and take me everywhere and get ma picture in the paper. 'Sooty finished the list.' Click. Everyone sending me their wishes and prayers. Prayers my arse. You up there? Are you fuckin listenin tae me, eh? Fuckin listenin tae any of this? Fuckin arsehole. Cunt. Why the fuck did you pick me, eh?

He laughs through the pain this is causing him.

Aye . . . eh. It's no finishin the list, that's what will really . . .

Not the fact I'll be shittin myself and pissin myself and throwin up over my Fred Perry's. I paid good money fur them.

He looks at his hair.

Losing my hair. The wan thing that makes me who I am?

Garry   You'll always be a fuckin ginge tae us.

They laugh and share a moment. **Garry** *pats his arm.*

Sooty   Anyways. Wits the point in cryin, eh? Fuckin man up?

He shakes this feeling and paints a smile on. Wipes the tears on his jacket.

Garry *looks to the audience.*

Paul *and* **Tubs** *enters.*

Tubs   Fuck me. It's no even gone twelve and yur being sick. Dirty bastard.

Sooty *doesn't respond.*

Paul   Here, ye see that fuckin wee belter of a lassie I've been dancin wie? Mate, she's a fuckin doll. Isn't she?

Sooty *ignores him.*

Paul   Gaz, go get him a water.

Garry   Right ye are.

Garry *steps to the side,* **Tubs** *fixes his hair in the mirror.*

Paul   Sooty, wits rang with ye?

Sooty   I've just been sick.

Paul   Naw, no that. Get over yurself aboot that. It's yur fucking face, Sooty.

Tubs   Aye, it has been trippin ye aw night, mate.

Sooty *takes a moment.*

Sooty   Paul . . . brother. You're . . . we've aw been pals since we were . . .

Paul *laughs at his drunk mess.*

Paul   Seven, yes . . . Right . . . Spit it oot, pishy heed.

Sooty (*struggling*)   Well, I just wanted to say how much I really . . . . . . I . . . I . . . lo . . . v . . .

He panics as **Paul** *looks at him.* **Sooty** *changes his mind revealing all.*

Sooty   I've got cancer.

Paul (*scoffs a laugh*)   Fuck up, naw you've no ya dafty, yur just pished /

Tubs *and* **Paul** *laugh. They look to* **Sooty** *and realise he isn't kidding.*

Tubs   Yur jokin, mate?

Paul   Aye, yur jokin, right?

Sooty *holds it in. He will not cry. He can't. The lads struggle on what to do. They say nothing. And hold the gaze.*

Tubs   Aye, but the . . . the doctors are fuckin amazin, Sooty? Int they? They'll sort it oot, mate. Right!

Sooty *nods.* **Paul** *stands in shock.*

Tubs   Mon, pal. Let's get ye hame.

Sooty   Hame? Wit ye sayin hame fur? That ABBA mega mix husny came oan yit.

Sooty *turns to exit.* **Tubs** *looks at* **Paul** *who is frozen still.*

Sooty   Hawl. Mon. Let's Voulez Vous.

Sooty *and* **Tubs** *exit leaving* **Paul** *and* **Garry***.*

Garry *to the audience.* **Garry** *passes* **Paul** *a Bucky bottle.*

Garry   'It canny be. He's just a boy' was everyone else's reaction. News travelled aroon fast. Everybody knew before the week wis up. You'd pass people in the street and they go 'Heard about Sooty . . . cancer is it?'

'AYE!' Aye, it's fuckin cancer. And wit? He's gonna get there wie it.

Every time he'd step in the pub folk ask him, or they pat him oan the back or you fuckin hear folk whisperin and pointin 'Cancer . . . awwk, it's a shame.'

Paul *stands. He starts to change into his strip. His body battered.*

Garry   It hit him hard. Paul imagined us aw growin auld together and still meetin doon the pub with oor flat caps and pipes, but deep doon, way . . . way deep doon, he knew Sooty wouldn't be a part of that, and that changed Paul. It really changed him.

Scene 11

JOBBY

Paul *takes off his top. His back is covered in belt lashes and bruises.*

Paul   Christ. You're early

Tubs   So are you . . .

They share a look.

Paul   Yur da?

Tubs   Aye. Yur da?

Paul   Aye. So . . . Where ye gonna go?

Tubs   My gran, if ye can believe it, says I can go roon hers for while.

Paul   Right.

The boys are heard outside the chaning room.

Tubs   Paul, before they come in . . . are you eh . . . aboot the whole Sooty thing . . . I know wit Sooty means tae ye, mate and . . . I am . . . here if . . .

Paul   Who we playin the day, mate?

Tubs *takes a beat. He knows* **Paul** *is knocking back his offer to be vulnerable.*

Tubs   Kilmarnock . . .

Eveyone enters.

The boys stand in their kits. **Mince** *is walking about holding his belly trying to hide the pain. There is tension. Nerves.*

Garry   Mornin. Right. Mince is finally getting a game.

They cheer half arsed.

Garry   Sooty is here . . . but he . . . eh . . . well, just needs tae take the next few weeks easy. Don't ye, buddy?

Sooty   Aye, I've goat the water and the sponge bucket if we need it. It is warm so just try . . . and . . . eh . . . keep . . . cool . . .

Garry   The team is Kilmarnock. No a bad . . .

The boys start coughing and moaning.

Garry   Eh . . . bunch . . . Right! Who the fuck wis that? That stinks.

Mince   Sorry boys. Ma nana made egg sandwiches . . .

Noodles   Fuck sake, Mince, ya fud.

Mince   But it's the nerves and that.

Tubs   That's fuckin hummin, ya dick.

Mick   Evacuate now!!!

They start to leave the changing room.

Garry   Right, everyone get oot and start warmin up. A three–nil lead by holf time. Mince. Move yur eggy arse.

Mince   Aye, right sorry. Just let me jump to the . . .

Oh no . . . oh fuck . . . I'm . . . gonna . . . myself . . . Fuck . . . Naw . . . fuck fucking

Mince *is left himself. He runs into the changing room cubicle. We hear a sigh of relief as he just makes it on time.*

Garry   Sorry about this . . .

Mince *is alone. He shouts like a wee child asking for more toilet roll.*

Mince   Fuck sake. Boys . . . anyone still in? Can someone get me some toilet paper? Boys . . . hello?

He panics and starts feeling about the cubicle. Head pops out. He spots the sponge bucket. His eyes light up . . .

Fuck me, man.

He shuffles with his pants trying to cover his front. He reaches into the sponge bucket. He washes his arse and drops the sponge back into the bucket and pulls up his shorts. A sigh of relief.

He closes the changing room door.

Sooty *re-enters for the bucket.*

Sooty   Mince. That is fucking horrible. Mon, get oot there.

He walks away . . . With the bucket.

Mince   But Sooty . . .

He runs to catch up with **Sooty**. *We are outside. On the pitch.*

Mince   Sooty / the bucket /

Noodles *jogs over.*

Noodles   Fuck sake, it's roastin. Go gee me a wee soak of that sponge before we start, Sooty.

Sooty   Aye, sure thing.

The sponge is slapped onto **Noodles**' *face. Brown shit is smudged across it. The boys stop and take a huge in-breath.*

Silence.

Mince   It was the egg sandwiches.

Noodles   MINCE!!!

Mince *runs and* **Noodles** *chases him.* **Garry** *to audience.*

Garry   Noodles got called jobby heed fur weeks. It took the attention aff Sooty fur a bit. God, every time he seen Noodles he would piss himself.

Chanting tae him

Chorus   Jobby heed. Jobby heed!

Garry   It was brilliant tae see Sooty laughin. Noodles didn't even mind because he knew it wis makin Sooty laugh ye know.

That's the thing aboot my boys. Always makin the best oot of a . . . shite situation . . .

Scene 12

MAD MAN

The set moves back to the pub. The lads sit with pints.

Mick   So when will you move then?

Noodles   Three weeks. So gonna huv tae rent a wee flat doon there as well. But the company will help wae that.

Garry   Fuck sake, man. Don't be comin back wae wan of those fuckin accents but.

Mick (*terrible cockney accent*)   Awrite, laddy. You coming down the boozer for a few jars.

Noodles   It's no fuckin *Only Fools and Horses*.

Tubs   Or *Treasure Island*.

Noodles   Aye, well, I am oot of this shitehole.

Mick   Leaving us cunts behind, eh Paul?

Sooty   And takin that big posh Filofax with ye, ya mad yuppie.

Tubs   Jealous of you, mate.

Mick   Wit ye sayin, Paul? That's him officially a posh London, English bastard now, eh?

Garry   Christ sake. English. Fuck that. Imagine being English.

Sooty   Would be shite.

Noodles   Oh aye, awful.

Mince   AYE. I would kill myself.

Beat. They look to him. And move on.

Mince   Here Paul, wit dae ye make of aw this then? Mad turncoat bastard over here.

Paul *looking away.*

Paul   Chuffed for you, mate.

We can see **Paul** *isn't pleased, someone is getting out of the town and he feels left behind. This reads in his face. The other lads feel it too. He drinks.*

Mince   Company wheels as well, is it?

Noodles   Aye.

Garry   Fuck sake, man. Imagine huvin yur ain motor.

Paul   Wit's the point in him huvin a motor . . . he canny drive?

Noodles   Well I can learn.

Paul   Well I wis just sayin wit's the point in a motor if you canny drive?

Noodles   Aye and I was just sayin I can learn, is there a problem with me getting this job or somethin, Paul?

Mince   Awwk wheesht, he'll learn nae bother. Just think . . . The freedom. Independence. Life on the auld road. Pickin up the birds. 'In ye get, darlin . . . dark car park, bish bash, get it up ye.'

Noodles   Awwk, sit doon.

Tubs   That's no way tae treat a lady.

Mince   Come back tae me when you've seen a lady, Tubs.

Tubs   Even I huv had more burds than you nan's made you hot dinners, mate. Noodles can be oor personal . . . wit dae ye call it fancy word fur driver

Mince   Chuffer. (*Says it wrong.*)

Sooty   It's chauffeur.

Noodles   Like hell I will. Sooty drives. He can gee ye a lift.

Tubs   Aye, drivin a moped isny real drivin but.

Sooty   Aye it is.

Mick   Wit use is it, but? Canny pick up burds.

Sooty   Well actually, I've hud a few lassies on the back of that scooter.

Tubs   Lies. Huv ye fuck. We are the mods. We are the mods.

Sooty   Fuck up you. And actually, aye a huv.

Mick   Who huv you picked up oan that thing, then?

Sooty   You won't believe me.

Tubs   Aye yur right, we won't . . .

Mick   Who?

Sooty   Naw, naw, a gentleman never tells.

Noodles   You are no a gentleman.

Mick   So get it telt.

Mince   Aye. Get it telt. Who you bend over that scooter, boy?

Noodles   Yur maw.

The boys laugh.

Mince   Ma maw's deed . . .

Pause.

Noodles   Oh aye, forgot about that, Mince.

Silence.

Noodles   Fucking hurry up and tell us who.

Sooty   Awrite. It . . . wis . . . Jennifer Melville.

Noodles   Did ye fuck pump big jugs Jenny!

Sooty *sits smug.*

Sooty   Yes indeedo.

Garry   Talk shite, Sooty.

Paul   Let me look in yur eyes. I can always tell when you're lying.

Tubs   Look in his eyes, who are you, fuckin Mystic Meg.

Paul *looks in his eyes.*

Paul   You dirty scooter boy bastard.

Garry   He did dae it as well!

Sooty   Aye, she wis standin outside her work, ye know she works part time doon at the chemist oan that make up bit and I hud just went in fur my prescription and I went

'Awrite Jen'

and she went

'Aye, Sooty. Yurself'

and I went

'Aye'

and she went

'You still dying'

and I went

'Aye'

and she went

'Awwk, that's a shame.'

Then we gave each other ye know . . . wan of they looks like . . .

He gives a flirty look.

Sooty   And then she went

'Wanty run me hame? A finish in five'

and I said

'Aye . . . I shall get the bike ready.'

And then she came oot and pure looked me in the eyes and went

'You're welcome'

and I went

'You're welcome? How am I welcome? I'm taking you home?'

and she went

'Aye, well I'm taking for fur a ride and it's probably gonna be the last ride you are ever gonna get . . .'

The boys laugh. As the bell of the pub goes. They all look apart from **Mince** *who is still laughing and drinking his pint.*

The lads eyes follow through the pub.

Mick   Fuck boys . . . boooys . . . It's him. Heeds doon.

Tubs   Oh Christ. Wit's he back here fur?

Noodles   Naw. That's no him, is it?

Tubs   Aye, Noodles. Wouldn't mistake him anywhere.

Garry   Dae ye think he's seen us looking.

Mick   If we aw keep starin then aye. Heads doon.

Noodles   Mad. Psycho. Bastard.

Mince (*loud*)   Who is it?

All   SHHHHH.

They pull him doon.

Noodles   It's Ian McDade fae that team in Greenock.

Mince   So? Wits the deal wie him?

Tubs   How do ye no know him? He's wan of the biggest gangsters aboot, Mince! He runs the fuckin town, mate. Drug cartel, murders. The lot.

Mince   Oooohhh scary. Wits the point?

Garry   We are playin his team on Saturday.

All the boys look at **Garry.**

Mick   We are wit?

Mince   I still don't get why that's a . . . (*Loud.*) Shit. Look at his face.

All the boys duck. They can't be seen.

Paul   Keep yur voice doon, dozy prick.

Mince (*loud as the sentence goes on*)   Sorry! But, you see that fuckin scar on his fuckin face.

Mick   Our point exactly. Keep yur fuckin voice doon, Mince.

Tubs   He's a mad man.

Noodles   He cut aff Wee Deccy Millar's leg.

Mince (*shouting now*)   THAT WAS THAT GUY!

They all duck again.

All   SHHHHH.

Paul   Shut the fuck up, ya wallaper.

Noodles   Aye, but they never proved it in court. Something tae dae with wan of the witnesses going missing or something.

Mince   Naw, I canny believe you've just telt me we are playin a crazy cunt that chops folks' legs aff on Saturday . . . NOPE. I'm oot.

Sooty   Stop being a shite bag, or you'll make me play.

Mick   Look, boys . . . Loooook . . . He's coming this way past . . .

The boys all look away. They try to look busy in order to not make contact with Ian.

Mick *whistles.* **Noodles** *hums a song.* **Garry** *talks about the karaoke on Thursday nights.* **Paul** *crawls out from the bar.* **Tubs** *ties his shoe.* **Sooty** *just finds it all funny but looks away.* **Mince** *is frozen still.*

Tubs   Away through the back aswell. Sleekit bastard.

Noodles   Thank fuck he's away, man. His presence wis making my pint stale, man.

Garry   Aye. He tends tae dae that.

Mick   Like the reaper, isn't he?

Garry   And his team is fuckin worse. Hawl, Mince. 999 oan the fuckin phone.

They drink up. **Mince** *is in shock.*

Mince   WIT!!! Wit dae ye mean the team is worse? Gaz? Tubs? MICK? Lads? . . .

Mince *continues stressing as the boys re-enter for the match. The pub moves to the changing rooms.*

Scene 13

MATCH

All the lads enter the changing room.

Mince   Lads . . . LADS. Listen up. Apparently, Ian McDade hates folk fae Paisley, right, no . . . I don't want tae cause yous undue concern, but we were all born in the Royal Alexander Hospital, that's IN PAISLEY, boys. If he finds that oot we are FUCKED, dae ye hear me, FUCKED.

Tubs   Aw Mince, mate, will ye gee it a fuckin rest. We were windin ye up, mate.

Noodles   Look at him shiting himself again . . .

Tubs   Says you, Jobby Heed.

Sooty   HA YAS! Jobby Heed! Jobby Heed!

Mince   As if we are playing Ian Scarface McDade.

Noodles   I know, mate. Say your prayers now, lads.

Tubs   Dear Jesus . . .

Paul   Shut up. None of that prayin shite anyways. Mince will start greetin if we make fun of it.

Mince   Dae wit ye want. It's no me that will burn in hell, bunch of proddy bastards.

Tubs   Wake up, Mince, this is hell.

Mick   Father, son and the holy load of shite.

Garry   Right, Fannies. Listen up here a minute! This is a feisty wan. Seriously, watch yur ankles oot there, boys. They love tae break a bone or two.

Let's go boys.

Scene 14

FIRST HALF

'One Step Beyond' by Madness plays. They all huddle and begin the movement. This is a real football match. The first time we have seen them play. Over the match **Sooty** *takes to the mic and pretends to be a posh, English football commentator.*

Sooty   Beautiful sunny day here in Greenock. You don't get to say that very often. Greenock versus Moorcroft.

(*Whistle.*)

Tubs with a clean slide tackle.

Over to Mince.

Through on goal.

And he's shot the other way! What the fuck, Mince?

Back to Mince. Chips it to Paul. Heads it across. Tubs is in. GOAL! One nil Moorcroft.

(*Whistle.*)

Greenock gets us back underway.

Mince for the tackle and he shites himself.

Mick picks up the loose ball. Noodles loses it but here come Greenock, Ian McDade, takes on one, two, three . . . chance . . . beautiful save by Gazza!

Long throw

Mick

Two–nil

Greenock get started once more (*Whistle.*)

Noodles intercepts, he's in the box, he's clipped at the heels.

Mince *gets punched in the face.*

Sooty Penalty!

Ohh . . . ouch from Ian McDade!

Mince *gets sent off and* **Sooty** *comes on the pitch.*

Sooty Don't discriminate against the fuckin cancer patient. This penalty is mine, boys.

Sooty *unzips his parka, but keeps it on. He takes the ball. Whistle. Silence.*

The boys follow the ball through the air. Slow motion. Whistle and they erupt.

Scene 15

HALF TIME

All the lads jog back to the changing room. Through the doors we hear **Ian** *screaming at the other team.*

Ian McDade (*V/O*)   They are fucking three–nil up! FUCKING three–nil. This is fucking piss poor. PISS POOR. They are winning in pink fucking strips, with one man down, a big poof, a wee Black bastard and one of their boys has FUCKING CANCER!!!

Mince   And a broken nose, Ian. Fucking team's broken it.

Mick   It's no broken. It's just bleedin.

Mince   Naw Mick, it's broken. I canny smell.

Tubs   Mince, breaking yur nose has nothin tae dae with smellin.

Mince   Aye, it does. And I canny smell. Thus my nose is broken.

Noodles   This just feels fuckin amazin. Doesn't it. Aw this. Us. Dain this.

Sooty   Too right!

Garry   We canny let it slip in the second hof, but lads.

Garry   Aye, that's right. Let's finish the bastards. Sooty, you alright to play on?

Sooty   Aye, Gaz.

The boys all cheer.

Garry   Good man. Let's fuckin dae this, boys.

All   Mon the fucking Croft.

Second Hof

'London Calling' by The Clash plays. They kick off again, this time **Mince** *is commentating and* **Sooty** *is playing.*

Mince   Second hof!

(*Whistle.*)

Noodles to Mick, Mick up the park and he misses. Even I'd score that . . .

Greenock up the park, beats Noodles. Great save from Garry, Sooty clears it.

(*Whistle.*)

Corner kick from Greenock. Here come Moorcroft, Noodles . . .

Scene 16

NOODLES

One player drops down. It's **Noodles**.

The boys in slow motion turn back and head towards their man on the ground.

Garry *steps out to the audience.*

Garry   We thought it was Sooty. Thought the fuckin cancer hud goat him there and then. But it wusny.

How can somebody just go, lit that.

The boys lift **Noodles** *off stage, like holding a coffin.* **Garry** *watches him go.*

Garry   He was fit, healthy. He was getting out of this place. Proper job. Office job. Going fuckin places, no like the rest of us . . . He wore suits for fuck sake . . .

He was bouncin aboot the changin room before. Buzzin to win this.

'Feels fucking amazin. Doesn't it. Aw this. Us. Dain this.'

I just don't get it. I still don't get it

Pause.

Scene 17

ROBBIE PARK

Mick *pulls a note and reads.*

Mick   Yur maw asked me tae read at the thing but I was too much of a shitebag.

So I thought I wid dae it here. Place we met. As wee kiddies. Wee boys playin fitbaw in the park. I hated ye because ye hud a new Rangers tap oan and a birthday badge. 'Aye that's him just turned six now.'

Paul *enters with a bottle. Half cut already.*

Mick   I thought six and he's goat a fuckin birthday badge. Wit a wanker.

He scrunches the note and shoves it in his pocket.

Aye. Some memories.

Paul *interrupts,* **Mick** *jumps at his voice.*

Paul   / Mind that time he did a naked lap aroon this park?

Mick   Paul . . .

Paul *(ignoring him)*   We were playin dares and he goat wan tae go ask Debbie McCann oot and he shat it and said 'no' cause he fancied her /

Mick   / We all saw his Noodley pubies. The only wan who ever did that daft forfeit.

Beat.

Paul   Why did it happen, Mick?

Mick   I don't know.

Paul   People don't just fuckin . . . drap doon lit that. His face . . .

Mick   I know . . .

Paul   First Sooty wae the cancer. Then Noodles just fuckin kicks it?

He drinks.

Mick   Paul, I know yur strugglin.

Paul   / Aw no, I'm no strugglin wae this anymare, Mick. It's fuckin killin me, mate.

Everyone in my life just fuckin . . . goes. And I'm beginnin tae wonder is it ME? Am I fuckin cursin everybody? A fuckin disease. The grim reaper makin everybody's life a pure fuckin misery. 'Cause I'm no stupid. I see it. I see it aw . . . I'm the reason my dad's a cunt, Mick. He was a cunt because he hud tae deal wae me.

Mick   Naw . . . that's no true, come oan, calm doon.

Paul   That's what he calls me, Paul the Plague. Paul the fucking . . .

Mick   Shut up. None of this is oor fault, Paul. You think I'm sittin in this park fur the good of my health? Naw. I'm tryin tae just . . . think and work it oot.

Paul *ignoring him.*

Paul   But wit's the fuckin point in that, eh? We aw die anyways. Sooner rather than later apparently. So fuckin cheers tae that.

Mick   Stop that.

Paul   Am a wrang, Mick? Eh? Am I? 'Cause we aw just end up in the same place. A fuckin hole in the grun, wae a shitty wee heedstone saying some bullshit aboot the type of person we were.

Mick *is getting really angry with him now.*

Paul   And folk fae this wee town. We leave shite all behind.
We are nothing mate. Nae cunt is gonny remember fuck aw
aboot us.

He scoffs. Then laughs.

Fuck . . . Startin a fuckin fitbaw team . . . thinking it was
gonna be good fur us, aye? . . . Fuck sake . . . goat my hopes
up fur nothin.

Mick   Goat yur hopes up? Goat YUR fuckin hopes up.
Paul, look at me. You have no idea wit it was like fur me tae
step back oan that park after aw these years. For the first
time in ma life, I felt like I wis worth somethin again. Or fur
Sooty tae come every fuckin week not knowin when he'd
play his last game just tae see us aw enjoyin ourselves. It
didny get oor hopes up for nothin, it fuckin saved us

Paul   Saved us fae wit, Mick?

Mick   from dain this! Acting like this. Drinkin oor lives
doon the pan or endin up like every other fuckin arsehole in
this town. This . . . this is wit the world wants us to be. And
you are handin it tae them on a fuckin silver platter, so shut
up with the self fuckin pity, it dosny suit you.

Paul   Wit? You tryin tae say that I huvny fuckin hud a hard
time wae aw this, Mick? . . .

Mick   Christ sake. Everyone is havin a hard time, Paul! Me,
you, Tubs, fuckin Noodles's family . . . Sooty by Christ. Oor
boy is dying, for fuck sake. Have some perspective.

Paul   Aye but . . .

Mick   No, Paul. There is no 'but'. See this . . . this is yur
problem. You are selfish.

Paul   Wit the fuck did ye just call me?

Mick   Selfish. Stuck in yur way. It's your way or the fuckin
high way. 'Me me me.' Never listen to anyone else. Never
grown up.

Paul   The fuck you talkin aboot . . . I huv grown up. I huv /

Mick   / Well how come I've sat in that pub and heard ye chat the same shite for the last six years. Blame everyone else fur yur problems, moan aboot the whole fuckin world being against ye as if ye were the most hard done by person in the fuckin room.

Hiding it all in this 'I'm a fuckin big man' bravado. Like Tubs . . . calling Tubs a 'wee poof' behind his back . . . Did that make ye feel smart, aye? 'Cause everyone laughed? And don't think for a minute, I don't know wit ye say aboot me when I'm no there.

Paul   Oh come aff it . . . It was fuckin banter, Mick. Banter, changin room banter.

Mick   Callin me a wee Black bastard and mockin ma family, aye?

It fuckin hurt, Paul. You were supposed to be my mate and I was terrified of ye. You say the same things I hear oan the fuckin pitches fae other teams or wit me and my wee maw hear just walkin doon the fuckin street. It's no just 'changin room banter' fur me. That's ma whole fuckin life.

Paul *drinks again.*

Mick   Do you ever consider anyone else in anythin? When Noodles goat his promotion, ye couldn't be happy fur him. Face like a slapped arse 'cause it wasn't you in the lime light. Or when I found oot that my fitbaw career ended, I came into the pub looking fur yur support and ye just laughed at me. It was like ye were happy I hud failed.

You don't know wit that was like fur me, Paul. For a wee lad like me. That looks like me, tae huv a chance like that taken away . . .

Paul *looks to the floor.*

Mick   This town isny a shitehole, Paul. You look at it like it's a shitehole. You see it through gritted teeth, mate. It doesn't have to be that way.

Paul   Wit dae ye want? A fuckin roon of applause for cutting hair in a fuckin barber's, Mick?

Mick   I don't want tae end up in the grun wae naebody rememberin anythin aboot me and I know you don't want that fur yourself either. Everyone wants tae be counted for somethin. You huv more chances than I will ever have. You need to start looking at the world in a different way, mate.

Paul   Stop. I want it to stop. I want it all to stop. Just stop. STOP. STOP. STOP.

Paul *lunges for* **Mick** *with the bottle in his hand.*

Mick   Don't, you're not your da.

Paul *bursts. He wails. He falls to the floor.*

Mick *takes his face. A real vulnerability between two men.* **Mick** *lost on how to support him. He cuddles him on the floor.*

Mick   Paul, it's just the bevy . . . I want you back at trainin next week.

Paul *breaks free from the embrace. He opens the bottle and drops the lid.*

Paul   I've hung up ma boots, Mick. And that's just the way it fuckin is.

Paul *drinks the rest of the bottle. Struggling to take in the liquid. He flings the empty bottle to the floor.*

Scene 18

WAKE

Garry *turns to the audience.*

Garry   Paul never came back tae trainin. I told ye at the start when you met him to remember wit I said aboot him.

He stopped showin up at the pub, the bookies, the barber's
. . . so Mick started tae go up to his hoose . . . chappin oan
the door just to see if he wis there.

His da would turn him away 'Paul's not coming oot tae play.
Go away'. A few weeks later, Mick went up tae chap oan . . .
just to check again . . . and there wis the flashin blue lights
. . .

The lads lift **Paul** *off stage. Like a coffin. Another mate gone.*
Garry *watches.*

Garry   I think back oan it all the time. If we weren't too
busy thinkin aboot aw the other things going oan and took
time tae check in wae each other aboot everythin that hud
happened then . . . aye, things would huv been different.

But we'd never go fur a pint and start givin it 'lads, I'm
really struggling' because if ye did, you'd get laughed at.
And that was it. That was the problem. We never spoke . . .
so we never knew and that's what killed Paul.

So that's on us.

He turns back to the audience.

That's on all of us.

The boys enter the pub. Sitting looking glum.

Mince   I feel like we shouldny be drinkin. Given the
circumstances . . .

They all shoot him a look.

Mince   Sorry. Just though the . . . silence was awkward.

Tubs   It's a wake, Mince. It's hardly like folk are gonna be
dain the fuckin conga aroon the pub.

Mince   Sorry.

Garry   He would have fuckin hated this. Aw of us sitting
aroon. Moaping aboot.

Sooty   He'll be havin a go at us up there.

Tubs   Screaming at us, so he will.

Mince   Aye he's lit, 'I'm fuckin deed no get oan wae it ya dafties'.

They shoot him a look again.

But out of an emotional build up **Sooty** *laughs. The boys all begin to properly laugh.*

Mince   Think he is in heaven?

Tubs   Wit ye tryin to say? He's in hell?

Mince   Naw! Fuck sake. I'm just sayin 'cause he didny believe in aw that.

Sooty   Aye, he did!

Mince   Naw. He was a proddy and that. (*He says 'proddy' like it's a bad word.*)

Sooty   Protestants believe in heaven as well, Mince.

Mince   Naw they don't.

Tubs   Aye, they dae, Mince.

Mince   Naw, my nana said they aw burn in hell. Especially the huns and the gays and the lez /

Tubs   Did she say that, aye? Right. Well, yur nana's a . . .

Garry   TUBS.

Sooty   But yur nana. She's no serious. She's just been bigot.

Mince   Don't be calling my nana a bigot, Sooty.

Tubs   But wit she said there, Mince, wis bigoted.

Mince   Aww, fuck sake. How? How does it matter anyways? Billy, Tim. Green, blue, shite we aw die and we don't go anywhere.

Mick   So you are no Catholic, then?

Mince (*serious*)   Naw. I. am. Catholic.

Garry   But you just said ye die ye die. Catholics believe in heaven, Mince.

Mince   Shite.

Garry   Dae you believe in God?

Mince   No really.

Sooty   So you're a Catholic that dosny believe in God . . .

The boys are confused. **Mince** *is getting flustered.*

Mince   God is a cunt if he is real.

Tubs   Mince! You canny use the lord's name lit that.

Mince   Says you, hole licker. You abused the lord's name when ya shoved a cock up yur arse.

Mick   MINCE!

Mince   Well, so fuckin wit. I'm sick of you aw taking the piss oot a me fur everythin I dae! And ye can take this piss oot of this as well. 'God' if he's fuckin there and you believe in him or no, took two of my best mates away and gave one of them fucking canc . . .

Pause. He looks at **Sooty** *and* **Sooty** *laughs.*

Sooty   Cancer. Yes. You can say it, Mince. It's no a big bad sweary word that will dam ye tae hell.

Tubs   Sorry, are we just gonny skate over the fact Mince just called me a 'hole liker.'

They laugh.

Mince   Sorry, Tubs. Naw, I didny mean that, mate. I don't know wit came over me there.

Tubs   The Holy Spirit?

Mince *huffs and kisses the cross around his neck. The boys look even more confused.*

Sooty   HOLD FUCKING ON, HE'S GOAT THE CROSS ON?

Garry   Cunt's a Catholic but no a Catholic.

Mick   Hof a Catholic.

Sooty   Hof Catholic, dosny believe in God but wears a crucifix aroon his neck?

Mince   See that there, that wis Jesus. He is real. And he died for us aw . . . Plus it's a nice necklace.

Sooty   Do you fuckin listen in chapel?

Mince   Aye! . . . Well . . . to be honest. I just go fur the breed. That communion breed is fuckin class, man, I could eat a whole loaf of that.

The boys all drink and scoff at **Mince**.

Mick   Right well. Shall we.

All   Aye.

Mick   To Paul.

All   Paul.

Beat.

Garry   Naw. Fuck this. FUCK. THIS! You think they two would be wantin us tae sit oan oor fat arses, pure pining after them? This isnty how it's meant tae go, boys.

Tubs   So wit dae we do?

Garry   Exactly, Tubs. Wit dae we dae aboot it? No just sit here. We get back oot there or something? No let this fuckin toon get us doon again.

Mince   Memorial match. You know? Like raise money fur charity.

Let's say some charity tae dae wae heart attacks and that. My nan geez them bags of clothes aw the time tae charities for hearts or some shite. So that could be good, aye? And then maybe like a . . . is there charities fur like alcoholics and that kinda thing? Dunno but if there is we could hof the cash and oh. OMG . . . here . . . oh . . . here OH! See how in the lead up tae the match, we dae other fundraising stuff like we did in the first place. When we started this team. Like race nights, quiz nights, maybe a wee bit of the auld karaoke a fucking ceilidh, everyone loves a good ceilidh . . .

Garry   Mince . . .

Mince (*under his breath*)   Fine. Just an idea, Garry.

Mick   MINCE! That's actually a fucking excellent idea.

Garry   Aye!

Mince (*full of himself*)   I know. Here . . . I. Know. That's why I said it. Call me Albert.

Garry   Albert?

Mince   Aye, Eensteen. Albert Eensteen.

Garry   I couldny sit oan my arse any longer. The pub was becoming even mare depressin than the fuckin graveyards. So, this wis it. The lead up tae the big memorial fitbaw match.

Scene 20

KARAOKE

Tubs *and* **Mick** *stand on the bar with tea towels tucked in their shorts. They sing 'Making Your Mind Up' by Bucks Fizz. They rip the tea towels off like the music video. Everyone cheers.*

Scene 21

STAND UP

Mince *is next and he appears behind the bar with a terrible homemade sock puppet.*

Garry   We were supposed to have a stand up comedy night but . . . nobody laughed.

As **Mince** *storms off, he shouts.*

Mince   Fuck sake. Fucking thing took me fucking ages, idiots, man, fucking idiots.

Over **Garry***'s next speech, we see* **Sooty** *really laughing.* **Mick** *enters behind him and dresses him in the hairdresser's cape. He puts a hat on* **Sooty**.

Garry *to audience.*

Garry   It was brilliant. The amount of effort people were putting in tae raise the money fur it despite how shit the events actually were. People looked past that and saw wit we were tryin tae dae fur the boys. That's wit's class about a fuckin community like oors. It's everythin they would huv wanted. We were doing them fuckin proud that's for sure.

Scene 22

PASSING THE PARKA

Sooty *is sat still wrapped in his parka looking out over the River Clyde.* **Mince** *enters and slaps his head. He sits beside him.*

Mince   Knew you'd be sat here, ya baldy bastard.

Sooty   Just needed some air, mate.

Mince   Fat chance of gettin air doon the fuckin River Clyde, mate. Water sings with shoppin trolleys in it.

Sooty   Aye and who puts the trolleys in the water, Mince?

Mince   I did it once. It was usually Noodles.

They laugh.

Sooty   Overwhelmin.

Mince   Wit?

Sooty   Know wit I was thinkin when I was watchin you all at the ceilidh. Mind at school when we use to do it aroon Christmas time instead of P.E.?

Mince   Christ, aye. You'd shite yourself that a lassie wouldn't come up and pick ye and you'd be stuck dancin wae the Mrs Mackinnon, mind? Or when the lassies would pick and you'd get stuck wae someone pure sweaty.

Sooty   That wis the worst.

Mince   Not that you hud any problems getting picked. Everyone use tae fancy you, despite ye being a ginge.

Sooty *taps his head.*

Sooty   Probably even better now, eh?

They laugh.

Sooty   Some life innit, Mince.

Mince   Wit?

Sooty   I mean . . . we goat it good in some ways. Might no be big hooses with loads a money and famous fancy jobs but know wit? I wouldn't change it fur the world, mate. This. This has been perfect for me, mate.

Mince   This is a shite hole right, but it's oor shitehole. We are fuckin kings here if we want tae be, mate. I feel like a king here.

Sooty   Kings? Aye . . . pushin it there. A court jester might suit you mare.

Mince   Usual.

Sooty   Naw. You are a king, mate! Don't let anyone tell you different, right?

Beat.

Sooty   I didn't need to lift the cup.

Mince   Wits that?

Sooty   I said, I didn't need to see Brighton.

Mince   Naw.

Sooty *stands. Takes off his jacket and passes it to* **Mince** *who stands with him.*

Sooty   Gonny go up the road and get an early night. Big match the morra! It's fucking roastin, but. I canny walk hame with my jacket oan so go get Garry tae bring it fur me the morra.

Mince   Why?

Sooty *knows exactly what he is doing.* **Mince** *understands just as much.*

Sooty   Go oan. Make sure ye give it to him. Give it to Garry.

Mince *and* **Sooty** *share a look. This is his final parting. The parka is the last piece of him and with strength he hands it over.*

Sooty *makes his way to his exit. He looks over the Clyde one more time. He smiles. Warmth in his heart. A life well lived. He is truly happy.*

Mince *calls to him to say something final.*

Mince   Sooty . . . I . . .

Sooty   I love you, Mince, I love yous all.

Sooty *takes one last look at the view before turing back to* **Mince** *who is now in tears but trying to hide it.*

Sooty   Twelve o'clock sharp.

Mince   Right. Don't ye be fuckin late now?

Sooty   Mon the fucking Croft.

Sooty *smiles to him and exits through the pub door.* **Mince** *exits behind the bar. He bundles the parka into a ball.*

Scene 23

RECORDS

Lights up on **Garry**. *The stage nearly empty.*

He begins.

Garry   In ma room. Record player oan. Paul Weller. It's stickin wee bit 'cause I goat it oot a second hand shop. I'm actually gonny give it tae wee Sooty 'cause he loves Paul Weller. Mare than me.

Ma maw's knockin the door. I'm ignorin her. Ye know it's getting tae the good bit. She comes in anyways.

She's lookin at me. Pure lookin at me.

'Can you turn that aff, Garry. I need you to come doon stairs. Scott's here.'

Scott? Who? So, I'm up. Turning Weller aff. Walking doon stairs and it's . . . Mince.

Mince   Sit doon, Garry.

Garry   Wits going oan?

Mince   Just sit doon, mate.

We see **Garry***'s face as the parka is handed out.*

Mince   He wanted you to have it.

Garry   Naw.

Mince   Garry, mate.

He turns to look up to **Mince** *and the other boys still alive us enter.*

Garry   Naw. Naw. Fuckin stoap that. Get that fuckin jacket away. Get it back tae him. Fuck. FUCK! NAW!

His pace and breathing quickens. His anxiety attack strikes.

He starts to breathe fast and heavy. This time the boys are talking over the top. **Tubs** *stands speaking. Holding a photo of the team.* **Mince** *hangs* **Sooty***'s jacket over the bar.*

Scene 24

SOOTY

Tubs   Even when he was told that the treatments would affect the quality of his life and they might not work . . . That he could have a little longer with us and live better if he didn't take the treatments, he would still take them in hope that this one might just work. This was the fighter in him. Just like his fitbaw. Always wanted to win. Fuckin trooper . . . oh . . . sorry . . . Excuse me.

A wee mod

A best friend

A team mate forever. Thank you, Sooty mate.

Mick   We'll give you some extra time, Garry.

Extra Time

The boys exit. **Noodles, Paul** *then* **Sooty** *looks back and smiles for a second before also exiting from the P.E. benches at the side of the stage.*

Garry *alone onstage.*

Garry   Extra time? I needed a whole fuckin match tae start over again. It felt like the rest of ma life wis gonny be a fuckin penalty shoot oot. This canny be it. Can it?

Three of ma fuckin best mates gone. Just lit that? I mean . . . Wits next? We aw get fuckin struck by lightnin.

This canny be right? It's aw fuckin no right, man.

I just think 'Moorcroft'. Wit we set oot tae be wis mare just a few boys fae the schemes. We aw came intae this the gither. To change oor circumstances. To get oot the shitehole. And . . . and . . . I'm no saying it wis bad luck. 'Cause I don't believe in that shite /

/ It was just a good crowd of boys, a crackin crowd of boys. That hud mare than their unfair share of folk takin nae well or dying in such a small fitbaw team?

But I still canny help wonder, why?

Folk use tae ask if it wis something in the pipes under the pitch we played oan, cursing us, I mean that's mental talk, but I started to wonder, could it huv been? Because it wis aw too fuckin spooky. Why did it aw happen tae us? When we aw goat back the gither tae play fitbaw?

Death, and fuckin mare death when we were only tryin tae make somethin of oor fuckin lives, man. This doesn't happen tae rich folk. I know this dosny happen tae fuckin rich folk. I canny understoan why, but? WHY! FUCKING WHY!

He breaks. Trying to change the subject. Trying to call in his mates.

I still see Mince, Tubs and Mick. Oh aye, only ones left standing no.

We meet fur pints and that sometimes. All auld bastards now but. Sure, we are lads?

Silence. The stage is empty. **Garry** *runs around the space looking for his friends . . . All ghosts now.*

I said we are all auld now, sure we lads? Boys?

Silence. Panic begins to deepen.

Ye know . . . I still sit up at night, right and I talk tae them aw. I think aboot them aw and I still talk tae them like this. I don't get enough sleep and ma body is weak fur ma work and I'm knackered. I'm fuckin knackered aw the fuckin time man. I have nae energy tae dae anythin.

I question it aw the time. Same story. Never changes. So I question it again. Questions and mare fuckin questions and thoughts and made up situations goes aroon ma heed aw the fuckin time. Aw I dae is think bad thing are gonny happen tae the folk I love and can ye fuckin blame me, man? Other mornin right, I wis late fur ma work because I seen a fire engine at the bottom of the street, and I hud said tae myself if that turns left up the hill, that's going tae my hoose. My hoose is oan fire and my family are deed. Psychotic! I know it's fuckin psychotic, but that's how bad it is. My chest. Christ. It's like ma fuckin chest is being held by a massive claw. Grippin right roon ma lungs and ma heart and I canny breathe right. Oan pills fur it no. Calms the anxiety doon . . . apparently.

Fuck know. These mad people I needy see are like,

'Talk about the experiences, Garry. Work through the tough times, Garry and let them slip away, Garry.'

What the fuck? Who are these posh educated cunts telling me to let it aw slip away? How can you tell a person tae forget aw that?

I canny forget. I don't want tae forget, because it's the only fuckin memory I huv of them aw and soon as I forget it. They are gone. For good and I don't want them to be gone because . . .

Garry's *voice cracks. He can't fight back the emotion any longer. The bottle lid has popped.*

Because I miss them . . .

He wipes his face, almost itching the tears away, not wanting to acknowledge he's upset.

Christ. ugh.

Beat.

You don't know wit this does tae a man . . .

You don't know wit this does tae a person.

Stillness.

1980s has slowly faded away and we live in the now. The present. Fifty again. A life has been well lived.

Garry   Well . . . that's it. That's the lot. Told ye, no sparkly costumes . . . Happy fuckin birthday.

He picks up a photo that's sat on the bar from **Sooty**'s *wake. He takes it and walks with it.*

Sadness overwhelms him looking at his team. Over his next speech, the other boys enter the stage again. **Sooty** *picks up his jacket, he puts it on again. They all form the set up for the photo around* **Garry** *who remains in the middle. He watches his friends, now ghosts, float around him.*

Garry   I live wae regret oan my shoulders. I replay this over and over hopin the story will change . . . it dosny. It's still the same. At forty, at fifty and sixty . . . it will still be the same. Every birthday I feel guilt. How am I here and they are no? If they were here, maybe they would have done somethin of note wae their lives . . .

I just wanted them to feel important . . . because they were. So fuckin IMPORTANT.

They all laugh with him, alive for a single moment one last time, trying to arrange where to stand in the photo. They freeze still in time for the photo. **Garry** *takes a moment. He looks at his team. Proud.*

Garry   I miss them like hell.

Hope in his eyes. To the audience.

Mon the fuckin Croft!

A camera click and flash to blackout. 'That's Entertainment' by The Jam plays.

When the actors do the curtain call, no formal bow should take place. They should stand in the position as if posing for a football photograph and then clap out to the audience like at the end of a match. Shaking hands.

The lads exit leaving **Garry** *for one final moment. He lights a cigarette and he winks to the audience.*

Walks off. The lights fade. End.

Mon the Croft.